TEACHER'S PET PUBLICATIONS

LITPLAN TEACHER PACK
for
Harry Potter and the Sorcerer's Stone

based on the book by
J. K. Rowling

Written by
Marion B. Hoffman

© 2001 Teacher's Pet Publications
All Rights Reserved

This **LitPlan** on J. K. Rowling's
Harry Potter and the Sorcerer's Stone
has been brought to you by Teacher's Pet Publications, Inc.

Copyright Teacher's Pet Publications 2001

Only the student materials in this unit plan may be reproduced. Pages such as worksheets and study guides may be reproduced for use in the purchaser's classroom. For any additional copyright questions, contact Teacher's Pet Publications.

SOME PAGES IN THIS LITPLAN ARE INTENTIONALLY LEFT BLANK TO FACILITATE TWO-SIDED PRINTING

Table of Contents - Harry Potter And The Sorcerer's Stone

Introduction	7
Unit Objectives	11
Reading Assignment Sheet	12
Unit Outline	13
Study Questions (Short Answer)	17
Quiz/Study Questions (Multiple Choice)	38
Pre-reading Vocabulary Worksheets	77
Lesson One (Introductory Lesson)	99
Nonfiction Assignment Sheet	102
Oral Reading Evaluation Form	103
Writing Assignment #1	108
Writing Assignment #2	117
Writing Assignment #3	132
Writing Evaluation Form	109
Vocabulary Review Activities	135
Extra Writing Assignments/Discussion ?s	123
Unit Tests	139
Unit Resource Materials	167
Vocabulary Resource Materials	189

A Few Notes About The Author and the Books
J. K. Rowling

The author of the Harry Potter books is said to be a very private person. And she might have kept it that way had she not created the now-four, soon to be five, Harry Potter books. To say that these novels have achieved fantastic success is to understate the sensation of Harry Potter. A quick search of the hundreds of web sites now devoted to Harry Potter reveal a true phenomenon.

There seems to be no aspect of life that has not been touched in some way by Harry Potter books and related memorabilia. From *Time* to *TV Guide* to web sites to chat lines to television and radio show to hundreds of articles, books, trinkets, posters, and other paraphernalia, Harry Potter has suddenly become a part of our daily lives. There is no escaping him or the new world in which he lives.

The books are about a young boy who catapults from life with his aunt and uncle, the "perfectly normal" Petunia and Vernon Dursley, and their fat and extremely spoiled child, Dudley. One day he is living unhappily at 4 Privet Drive, and the next he finds that he is the child of the famous wizards, Lily and James Potter, and has been accepted at Hogwarts School of Witchcraft and Wizardry. Thus the adventures of Harry Potter begin.

J. K. Rowling, born Joanne Kathleen Rowling, in 1965 in Chipping Sodbury, England, is said to have written the first Harry Potter book on scraps of paper in a local café while her infant daughter Jessica slept nearby. A single parent and nearly destitute financially, Rowling created Harry Potter and his entourage mostly out of her own imagination and desires, with a wealth of magic, mythology, and other related sources tossed in.

Her success has been extraordinary. Not only have her books sold like the proverbial hot cakes, but they have achieved marked success by earning notable awards and other recognition.

Harry Potter and the Sorcerer's Stone has been a *New York Times* Bestseller, a *USA Today* Bestseller, a *Publishers Weekly* Best Book of 1998, *Booklist* Editor's Choice, and Winner of the 1997 National Book Award in the United Kingdom.

It has been, in addition, an ALA Notable Book, winner of the 1997 Gold Medal Smarties Prize, a New York Public Library Best Book of the Year for 1998, and recipient of the *Parenting* Book of the Year Award in 1998.

The Potter books so far as **Harry Potter and the Sorcerer's Stone**, **Harry Potter and the Chamber of Secrets**, **Harry Potter and the Prisoner of Azkaban,** and **Harry Potter and the Goblet of Fire.** A fifth book is due to be available soon.

About the Author - **Harry Potter** - page 2

It is not difficult to understand the popularity of the Potter books. Not only do children of varying ages delight in them, but adults too love them for their fantasy and escapism. Not only do the books rescue the inner child in adults, but they bring an escapism and a sense of hope to their daily lives.

No more sitting in traffic on the interstate wanting desperately to be at home: simply grab a broom and soar above the crowds on your merry way. No more putting up with bullies, people who can't tolerate differences, and "perfectly normal" folks: simply tap your wand, think good thoughts, and–presto!–your world is changed. Want your own bit of anonymity: toss on your invisibility cloak and go for it. Think of a moral universe in which good prevails over evil, in which the guys (and girls) in the white hats face challenges superbly and then reign supreme. This is the world of Harry Potter.

Think of a world in which Hermione Granger and Ron Weasley and the giant Hagrid are your best friends. Think of being able to rely totally on those friends. Think of having the wonderful Albus Dumbledore to consult and to rescue you. Think of having a new world of intrigue and fantasy opened to you. Think of having your team win, not just because of your athletic prowess, but because you do the "right" thing and demonstrate the "right" qualities. This is the world of Harry Potter.

That universe is not without its reality. The evil Voldemort will certainly return to fight another day. "Bad" people will continue to plague us. The dark side of life will never go away, and we constantly have to be on the alert for the very real problems with which life challenges us. But if we believe in Harry Potter, if we believe that there is hope, if we believe that we can rise to whatever challenges we face–then we have, at least in a small way, helped to right the universe and make it a better, happier place to live. We may have to spend some of our time with the Dursleys, but, in the end, we will always have Hogwarts in our hearts.

Introduction

This unit has been designed to develop students' reading, writing, thinking, and language skills through exercises and activities related to **Harry Potter** by J. K. Rowling. It includes twenty-one lessons, quizzes, worksheets, unit tests, and extra resource materials.

The **introductory lesson** introduces students to one of the novel's main themes (belonging) through a bulletin board activity. During the novel's introduction, students will learn how the board's activities relate to the book they are beginning to read. Depending on how long you can, or want to, keep the bulletin board intact in the classroom, you might want to keep referring to it to deepen students' thoughts about belonging, to a family, a group, a neighborhood, a region, or a country.

The twelve **reading assignments** vary significantly in length; the early assignments are one chapter long, but toward the end of the book, the assignments cover two chapters at a time. Students have approximately fifteen minutes of pre-reading work to do (a little longer for the three longer reading assignments) prior to each reading assignment. This pre-reading work involves reviewing the study questions for the assignment and doing some vocabulary work for the vocabulary words they will encounter in their reading.

The **study guide questions** are fact based: students can find their answers right in the text. The questions come in two formats: short answer or multiple choice. The best use of these materials is probably to use the short answer version of the questions as study guides for students (since answers will be more complete) and to use the multiple choice version for occasional quizzes.

The **vocabulary work** is intended to enrich students' vocabularies as well as to aid in their understanding of the novel. Prior to each reading assignment, students will complete a two-part worksheet for a number of vocabulary words in the upcoming reading assignment. Part I focuses on students' use of general knowledge and contextual clues by giving the sentence in which the word appears in the text. Students may then write down what they think the words mean based on their usage. Part II nails down the definitions of the words by giving students dictionary definitions of them and having students match the words to the correct definitions based on the words' contextual usage. Students should then have an understanding of the words when they meet them in the text. There are a total of 104 vocabulary words for the whole book.

After each reading assignment, students will go back and formulate answers for the study guide questions. Discussion of these questions will serve as a **review** of the most important events and ideas presented in the reading assignments.

Introduction - **Harry Potter** - page 2

A series of **extra discussion questions** is part of Lesson Twelve. These questions will give students an opportunity to use more critical thinking skills and should provide for some lively class discussions. Feel free to use these questions in whatever way seems most appropriate for your students. If you like, the extra discussion questions can become the basis for some **group activities**. They can be used at any time during your teaching of the novel: there is nothing magical about using them in Lesson Twelve.

The extra discussion questions focus on interpretation, critical analysis, and personal response, employing a variety of thinking skills and adding to the students' understanding of the novel. In fact, if your students enjoy classroom discussions, you might have them come up with additional questions for consideration.

The LitPlan for **Harry Potter** was created to give you lots of flexibility. You may use the plan as a self-contained guide to teaching the novel, but you will also find that it gives you the opportunity to define your classroom approach for yourself. Sometimes students can just work alone in and out of class, sometimes they can work in small groups, sometimes they will be giving and listening to reports, and sometimes the group as a whole will be focused on a classroom assignment or discussion that relies heavily on their participation. Lesson Thirteen, which affords an opportunity to do role playing, and Lesson Nineteen, which offers some vocabulary games the students may play, create an environment for students to work with each other.

After students complete extra discussion questions, there is a **vocabulary review** lesson which pulls together all of the fragmented vocabulary lists for the reading assignments and gives students a review of all of the words they have studied. (Note: Although **Harry Potter** is a very popular, interesting, and entertaining book, its vocabulary is relatively easy to read and understandable. Depending on your students' skills level, the words might prove not to be especially challenging to them. Should that be the case, you might like to use some of the vocabulary time having students come up with synonyms and antonyms for the vocabulary words. Maybe students could even play with using all vocabulary words from one reading assignment in a sentence. These sentences–some of them perhaps written mostly for fun–could be put on the board prior to class.)

There are three **writing assignments** in this unit. Through the writing assignments, students will become familiar with a variety of ways of organizing and expressing their thoughts. The first writing assignment, introduced in Lesson Six, is to inform/explain, but students will also have a discussion about not belonging. The second assignment, introduced in Lesson Ten, is to write a news story ostensibly based on the book. The third and final writing assignment, introduced in Lesson Twenty, gives students a choice of six different topics on which to write from personal opinion. By the time that they are in Lesson Twenty, they should have a thorough understanding of **Harry Potter** and be able to write a satisfactory paper from their own personal viewpoint.

Introduction - **Harry Potter** - page 3

There is also a **nonfiction reading assignment**. Students are required to read some nonfiction related in some way to **Harry Potter**. After reading their nonfiction pieces, students will fill out a worksheet on which they answer questions regarding facts, interpretation, criticism, and personal opinions. Students are also given the opportunity to make **oral presentations** about the nonfiction pieces they have read. This method not only exposes all students to a wealth of information, it also gives students a chance to practice **public speaking**.

There is an optional **class project** (Project Modern Magic) through which students gain some additional knowledge of modern magic and magicians. Feel free to use the entire project, to modify it, or to eliminate it altogether. You might even want to use parts of it to create extra credit projects.

Review lessons throughout the plan pull together all of the aspects of the unit. Not only will the reviews help students to connect all the threads of the novel, but they also will give you a clear picture of whether or not students have understood what they have read.

The **unit test** comes in three types: short answer, advanced short answer (more critical thinking), and multiple choice. Altogether there are five unit tests.

There are additional **support materials** in this LitPlan–**games, puzzles, bulletin board ideas, etc**. There are **answer keys** for most materials. As always, please feel free to use whatever appeals to you and will be supportive of your students' learning.

You are also being provided with two forms–an **Oral Reading Evaluation Form** and a **Writing Evaluation Form**–to use in any way you wish. Both forms may be used by you and/or by the students.

A final note: You know your students, yourself, and your school environment better than anyone else does. This LitPlan is designed to be supportive of you, not to restrict you in your own personal teaching style. The materials in this LitPlan are offered to complement your teaching style and to contribute to your students' optimal learning experience.

Unit Objectives - Harry Potter

1. Through reading and discussing **Harry Potter**, students will preliminarily gain a better understanding of the themes of belonging and not belonging. Students are also encouraged to consider such themes as bravery, revenge, courage, family values, friendship, greed, and loyalty. They are strongly encouraged to study the book carefully but also simply to enjoy it. And of course **Harry Potter** offers ample material to generate discussions of good vs evil.

2. Students will demonstrate their understanding of the text on four levels: factual, interpretive, critical, and personal.

3. Students will define and express their own viewpoints on the aforementioned themes.

4. Students will be exposed to several different points of view and will learn something about standing up for one's principles and being true to oneself and to others.

5. Students will learn about juvenile detention in their town and perhaps in their nation.

6. Students will be given the opportunity to practice reading aloud and silently to improve their skills in each area. They will from time to time receive feedback on their reading ability.

7. Students will answer questions to demonstrate their knowledge and understanding of the main events and characters in **Harry Potter** as they relate to the author's theme development.

8. Students will enrich their vocabularies and improve their understanding of the novel through the vocabulary lessons prepared for use in conjunction with the novel.

9. The writing assignments in this unit are geared to several purposes:
   A. To have students demonstrate their ability to write clearly and effectively in a variety of ways.
   Note: Students will necessarily use a variety of rhetorical devices in order to complete their writing assignments. If you like, you may mention on their writing that they have effectively used narrative, comparison/contrast, or whatever, even though they might not have been directed to use these particular devices in any given assignments.
   B. To check the students' reading comprehension
   C. To make students think about the ideas presented by the novel.
   D. To encourage logical thinking

Reading Assignment Sheet - Harry Potter

Date Assigned	Reading Assignment (Pages)	Completion Date
	Chapter One	
	Chapter Two	
	Chapter Three	
	Chapter Four	
	Chapter Five	
	Chapter Six	
	Chapter Seven	
	Chapter Eight	
	Chapters Nine and Ten	
	Chapters Eleven and Twelve	
	Chapters Thirteen and Fourteen	
	Chapters Fifteen and Sixteen	
	Chapter Seventeen	

Unit Outline - Harry Potter

1 Introduction to unit Distribution of materials for unit Bulletin board activity	2 Preview One	3 Begin theme discussion Read aloud One Evaluate reading Preview Two	4 Review One Read Two In-class activity (family and community dynamics)	5 Review Two Preview Three RA Three
6 WA #1	7 Review Three Paragraph writing Preview Four	8 Read Four Class discussion (Hagrid's presence) Preview Five RA Five	9 Review Five Class discussion (characters) Prep for NFRA.	10 Begin NFRA Assign WA #2 Preview Six RA Six
11 Review Six Set up class project Preview Seven	12 Read Seven Review all to date Use extra discussion questions	13 Assign preview Eight RA Eight Role-playing exercise	14 Review Eight Preview Nine and Ten Read Nine and Ten Oral reports NFRA	15 Oral reports NFRA Review Nine and Ten
16 Preview Eleven and Twelve Catch up on loose ends	17 Read Eleven and Twelve Preview Thirteen and Fourteen RA Thirteen and Fourteen Project reports	18 Continue project reports Preview Fifteen and Sixteen RA Fifteen and Sixteen	19 Preview Seventeen Read Seventeen	20 Review whole book WA #3
21 Vocabulary review for whole book	22 Unit Tests			

Key:

NFRA = Nonfiction Reading Assignment   Chapters expressed: One, Two, Three, etc.
RA = Reading Assignment
WA = Writing Assignment

STUDY GUIDE QUESTIONS

Short Answer Study Guide Questions - Harry Potter

Chapter One
1. What did the reader learn about Mr. and Mrs. Dursley in the book's first paragraph?
2. What did Mr. Dursley do for a living?
3. What big secret did Mr. and Mrs. Dursley want to keep?
4. What was the first unusual thing that Mr. Dursley thought he saw as he left for work?
5. What was unusual about the people Mr. Dursley saw while he waited in a traffic jam?
6. When he went to the baker's at lunchtime, whom did Mr. Dursley think he heard people talking about?
7. What unusual occurrences were mentioned that night on television news?
8. Who was the cat on Privet Drive **really**?
9. What person suddenly appeared next to the cat?
10. Why was Albus Dumbledore in the Dursley's neighborhood?
11. How did Hagrid arrive in the Dursley's neighborhood?
12. What did Harry Potter's scar look like?

Chapter Two
1. What dream was Harry having when his aunt woke him in the morning?
2. Where in the Dursley house did Harry sleep?
3. What was the first rule for a quiet life with the Dursleys?
4. Who got all of the good things in the Dursley household?
5. What was Dudley Dursley's complaint about his birthday presents?
6. Who was Mrs. Figg?
7. Why did Harry finally get to go to the zoo with the Dursley family?
8. What kind of strange things often happened around Harry?
9. What strange occurrence happened in connection with Harry at the reptile house?
10. What strange vision did Harry have about his dead parents?

Chapter Three
1. What was Dudley's favorite sport?
2. What was the difference in the schools Dudley and Harry were going to attend?
3. What was the difference in the two boys' school uniforms?
4. What was unusual about the mail that arrived at the Dursley residence the day before Harry's eleventh birthday?
5. Why did Mr. and Mrs. Dursley move Harry into a different bedroom?
6. What was in Harry's new bedroom?
7. What about Harry's second letter convinced Mr. Dursley that someone was watching the family?
8. Why did Mr. Dursley nail the mail slot shut?
9. Why did Mr. Dursley make everyone leave the house?
10. What strange thing happened at the hotel?

Study Guide Questions - **Harry Potter** - page 2

Chapter Four
1. Who arrived with a BOOM at the little shack?
2. What letter did Harry receive from Hagrid?
3. How did Hagrid communicate with Professor Dumbledore from the shack?
4. What were Muggles?
5. What did Harry learn about himself from Hagrid?
6. What did Harry learn about how his parents died?
7. Who was Voldemort?
8. What caused Harry's scar?
9. What did Harry remember for the first time about the night his parents died?
10. What magic did Hagrid strike Dudley with?

Chapter Five
1. How did Hagrid get to the shack in the middle of the water?
2. What was Gringotts?
3. Where was Gringotts?
4. Who ran Gringotts?
5. How were the high security vaults at Gringotts guarded?
6. What did Hagrid and Harry need to purchase in Diagon Alley?
7. What was the name of the pub Hagrid and Harry visited?
8. What was Professor Quirrell's most notable trait?
9. What did Hagrid pick up at Gringotts?
10. What was so unusual about the wand Harry got at Ollivander's?

Chapter Six
1. How did the Dursleys treat Harry when he returned home?
2. What was the name of Harry's owl?
3. From what platform did Harry's train to Hogwarts leave?
4. How did Harry get through to his train platform?
5. Who were Percy, Fred, George, and Ron Weasley?
6. Who did Harry meet for a second time at the train station?
7. Why did everyone at the train station stare at and want to meet Harry?
8. What were Bertie Bott's Every Flavor Beans?
9. Why didn't Ron buy anything to eat on the train?
10. What came inside the Chocolate Frogs that Harry bought?
11. What girl did Harry meet on the train?
12. Who lost and then found his toad on the train?

Study Guide Questions - **Harry Potter** - page 3

Chapter Seven
1. Who was the tall, black-haired witch in emerald-green robes who met Hagrid and the first-year students at the door of Hogwarts?
2. What were the names of the four houses at Hogwarts?
3. What was the purpose of the Sorting Ceremony?
4. Which house did the Hat choose for Harry?
5. What were the four words Professor Dumbledore spoke before the banquet at Hogwarts?
6. What was the real name of the ghost called "Nearly Headless Nick"?
7. What was the name of the Slytherin ghost?
8. What part of the Hogwarts grounds were forbidden to students?
9. Who was the Hogwarts caretaker?
10. What area inside of Hogwarts was out of bounds to everyone?

Chapter Eight
1. Who was the Potions Master at Hogwarts?
2. How many staircases were there at Hogwarts?
3. Who was always tricking first-year students at Gryffindor?
4. What was the name of Filch's cat?
5. What did the cat do?
6. Who was the dumpy little witch who teaches Herbology?
7. Who was Professor Flitwick?
8. What course did Professor Quirrell teach?
9. Who invited Harry to come to visit for a cup of tea?
10. Which professor picked on Harry in class?
11. Who was Fang?
12. What interesting news was found in the **Daily Prophet**?

Chapter Nine
1. What was the only class that Gryffindors and Slytherins took together?
2. What gift did Neville's grandmother send to him?
3. Who was the teacher for flying lessons?
4. What happened to Neville when he first flew?
5. How did Harry get chosen for the Quidditch team?
6. Who was Oliver Wood?
7. What was the password to get past the portrait of the fat lady?
8. Who challenged Harry to a duel?
9. How was Harry tricked about the duel?
10. What creature frightened Harry and his friends in the forbidden third-floor corridor?

Study Guide Questions - **Harry Potter** - page 4

Chapter Ten
1. What was in the long, thin package sent to Harry in the Great Hall?
2. How many players were on a Quidditch team?
3. What was the Quidditch ball called?
4. What was Harry's position on the Quidditch team?
5. When was a Quidditch match over?
6. How many points were awarded for catching the Golden Snitch?
7. Why didn't Harry and Ron return to their dormitory when they heard about the troll?
8. In what room did Harry and Ron lock the troll?
9. What were the words of the spell that Ron used on the troll?
10. Who took the blame when Professor McGonagall found that Ron, Harry, and Hermione were not in their dormitory?

Chapter Eleven
1. What book about Quidditch did Hermione lend to Harry?
2. What did Harry see happening between Snape and Filch?
3. What did Hermione do to Snape when she thought he was putting a spell on Harry's broomstick?
4. How did Harry win the Quidditch game for the Gryffindors?
5. What was the score of the game that Gryffindor won against Slytherin?
6. What name did Hagrid inadvertently give to Harry, Ron, and Hermione?

Chapter Twelve
1. As Christmas approached, how was Malfoy taunting Harry?
2. How did Ron, Harry, and Hermione try to find out about Nicolas Flamel?
3. What was the name of the librarian at Hogwarts?
4. How was wizard chess different from regular chess?
5. What Christmas gifts did Harry receive?
6. How did Harry decide to test the invisibility cloak?
7. What did Harry see in the Mirror of Erised?
8. What did Professor Dumbledore say the mirror showed people?

Chapter Thirteen
1. Who was the referee for the home championship Quidditch game?
2. What curse was put on Neville by Malfoy?
3. How did Harry finally remember having read something about Flamel?
4. What was said about Flamel in Hermione's book?
5. What was the Sorcerer's Stone said to be able to do?
6. What did Malfoy constantly taunt Ron about?

Study Guide Questions - **Harry Potter** - page 5

7. How did the championship Quidditch game end?
8. How long did the championship Quidditch game last?
9. What interaction did Harry think he had witnessed between Snape and Quirrell?
10. Why was Harry not interested in the victory party in the Gryffindor common room?

Chapter Fourteen
1. What did Hermione keep nagging Ron and Harry to do?
2. What was Hagrid looking up in the library?
3. What was Hagrid keeping illegally in his hut?
4. Who knew how to get past Fluffy?
5. What was in the huge black egg in the middle of the fire in Hagrid's hut?
6. Who looked in the window and saw the dragon at Hagrid's?
7. What was the dragon's name?
8. How did Ron, Harry, and Hermione get the dragon out of Hogwarts territory?

Chapter Fifteen
1. What did Professor McGonagall say that lessened somewhat the severity of Harry, Hermione, and Neville's actions?
2. Why did Harry suddenly become one of the most hated students at Hogwarts?
3. What were the students supposed to find in the forest?
4. What were the beasts in the forest who were part man and part horse?
5. How was Harry rescued from the cloaked figure who drank the unicorn's blood?
6. What was the note that Harry found pinned to the invisibility cloak when it was returned to him?

Chapter Sixteen
1. How were the written exams bewitched?
2. What were the practical exams?
3. Who gave away the secret of how to get past Fluffy?
4. Why did Harry decide to risk going after the Sorcerer's Stone himself?
5. How did Hermione keep Neville from going with her, Ron, and Harry to seek the Stone?
6. How did Harry, Ron, and Hermione get past Peeves?
7. What immediately put Fluffy to sleep?
8. What did Ron and Harry fall into when they dropped through the trap door?
9. What were the objects that looked like small, jewel-bright birds?
10. What did Ron, Hermione, and Harry have to do to get past the chessboard?

Study Guide Questions - **Harry Potter** - page 6

<u>Chapter Seventeen</u>
1. What was Harry's great revelation about Snape and Quirrell?
2. Who was Quirrell's master?
3. How did Harry wind up in possession of the Sorcerer's Stone?
4. Where did Harry see Voldemort's face revealed?
5. How was Quirrell kept from doing a curse on Harry?
6. What ultimately happened to the Sorcerer's Stone?
7. Why was the Sorcerer's Stone ultimately not such a wonderful thing?
8. How did Harry's mother's love for him protect him against Quirrell?
9. Why had Professor Snape tried to protect Harry?
10. How had Harry managed to get the Sorcerer's Stone out of the mirror?
11. What present did Hagrid bring to Harry in the hospital wing?
12. How did Gryffindor wind up winning the house cup?
13. Which student was most surprised at being awarded points?
14. Why did Harry say that he would actually have a good holiday with the Dursleys?

Key: Study Guide Questions - Harry Potter

<u>Chapter One</u>

1. What general information did the reader learn about Mr. And Mrs. Dursley in the book's first paragraph?
   They were "perfectly normal" people.

2. What did Mr. Dursley do for a living?
   He was the director of Grunnings, a firm which made drills.

3. What big secret did Mr. And Mrs. Dursley want to keep?
   They wanted to keep Mrs. Dursley's sister a secret.

4. What was the first unusual thing that Mr. Dursley thought he saw as he left for work?
   He thought he saw a cat reading a map.

5. What was unusual about the people Mr. Dursley saw while he waited in a traffic jam?
   The people were strangely dressed in cloaks.

6. When he went to the baker's at lunchtime, whom did Mr. Dursley think he heard people talking about?
   He thought he heard people talking about the Potters and their son Harry.

7. What unusual occurrences were mentioned that night on television news?
   Owls flying in the daytime and a downpour of shooting stars instead of rain were mentioned.

8. Who was the cat **really**?
   The cat really was Professor McGonagall.

9. What person suddenly appeared next to the cat?
   Albus Dumbledore appeared.

10. Why was Albus Dumbledore in the Dursley's neighborhood?
    He had come to bring Harry Potter to his aunt and uncle.

11. How did Hagrid arrive in the Dursleys' neighborhood?
    He arrived out of the air on a huge motorcycle.

12. What did Harry Potter's scar look like?
    His scar looked like a bolt of lightning.

Key - Study Questions - **Harry Potter** - page 2

Chapter Two
1. What dream was Harry having when his aunt woke him in the morning?
   He was dreaming about a flying motorcycle.

2. Where in the Dursley house did Harry sleep?
   He slept in the cupboard under the stairs.

3. What was the first rule for a quiet life with the Dursleys?
   Don't ask questions.

4. Who got all of the good things in the Dursley household?
   Dudley Dursley, Harry's cousin, got all the good things.

5. What was Dudley Dursley's complaint about his birthday presents?
   He complained that he didn't get enough of them.

6. Who was Mrs. Figg?
   She was a mad, old lady who lived two streets away from the Dursleys.

7. Why did Harry finally get to go to the zoo with the Dursley family?
   His aunt and uncle weren't able to think of anything else to do with him.

8. What kind of strange things often happened around Harry?
   His hair was cut and grew back overnight; his sweater shrank all on its own; and he was able to leap onto a chimney.

9. What strange occurrence happened in connection with Harry at the reptile house?
   A snake communicated with him, then the glass front on the snake's tank vanished, and the snake was able just to slither away.

10. What strange vision did Harry have about his dead parents?
    He saw a blinding flash of green light and had a burning pain on his forehead.

Chapter Three
1. What was Dudley's favorite sport?
   It was Harry Hunting.

Key - Study Questions - **Harry Potter** - page 3

2. What was the difference in the schools Dudley and Harry were going to attend?
Dudley was to attend Smeltings, an old private school; Harry was to attend Stonewall High, the local public school.

3. What was the difference in the two boys' school uniforms?
Dudley had a brand new uniform; Harry had some of Dudley's old things dyed gray.

4. What was unusual about the mail that arrived at the Dursley residence the day before Harry's eleventh birthday?
A letter arrived addressed to "Harry in The Cupboard Under the Stairs."

5. Why did Mr. and Mrs. Dursley move Harry into a different bedroom?
It was clear that someone watching them knew that Harry lived in a cupboard.

6. What was in Harry's new bedroom?
All of Dudley's discarded things and his unread books were in Harry's new bedroom.

7. What about Harry's second letter convinced Mr. Dursley that someone was watching the family?
The second letter was addressed to "Harry in The Smallest Bedroom."

8. Why did Mr. Dursley nail the mail slot shut?
He nailed it shut so that no mail could be delivered.

9. Why did Mr. Dursley make everyone leave the house?
More and more letters addressed to Harry arrived at the house.

10. What strange thing happened at the hotel?
Hundreds of letters arrived addressed to "Harry in Room 17 of the Railview Hotel."

Chapter Four

1. Who arrived with a BOOM at the little shack?
Rubeus Hagrid, Keeper of Keys and Grounds at Hogwarts arrived.

2. What letter did Harry receive from Hagrid?
He received a letter of acceptance at Hogwarts School of Witchcraft and Wizardry.

3. How did Hagrid communicate with Professor Dumbledore from the shack?
He sent Dumbledore a letter via owl.

Key - Study Questions - **Harry Potter** - page 4

4. What were Muggles?
   Muggles were Nonmagic folk

5. What did Harry learn about himself from Hagrid?
   He learned that he, Harry, was a wizard.

6. What did Harry learn about how his parents died?
   He learned that his parents died by being blown up, not by being killed in an automobile accident.

7. Who was Voldemort?
   He was a wizard gone bad.

8. What caused Harry's scar?
   Voldemort caused the scar when he tried to kill Harry.

9. What did Harry remember for the first time about the night his parents died?
   He remembered hearing a high, cold, cruel laugh.

10. What magic did Hagrid strike Dudley with?
    He gave Dudley a curly pig's tail which stuck right through Dudley's pants.

Chapter Five

1. How did Hagrid get to the shack in the middle of the water?
   He flew there.

2. What was Gringotts?
   Gringotts was a wizard bank.

3. Where was Gringotts?
   It was hundreds of miles under London, deep under the Underground.

4. Who ran Gringotts?
   It was run by goblins.

5. How were the high security vaults at Gringotts guarded?
   They were guarded by dragons.

Key - Study Questions - **Harry Potter** - page 5

6. What did Hagrid and Harry need to purchase in Diagon Alley?
They needed to purchase school supplies for Harry (uniform, books, a wand, a cauldron, a set of phials, a telescope, a set of brass scales, and–optionally–an owl OR a cat OR a toad).

7. What was the name of the pub Hagrid and Harry visited?
It was "The Leaky Cauldron."

8. What was Professor Quirrell's most noticeable trait?
He stuttered.

9. What did Hagrid pick up at Gringotts?
Hagrid picked up something referred to as "the You-Know-What in vault seven hundred and thirteen."

10. What was so unusual about the wand Harry got at Ollivander's?
The tail feather in Harry's wand belonged to a phoenix who gave a second tail feather to the wand belonging to Voldemort.

Chapter Six
1. How did the Dursleys treat Harry when he returned home?
They mostly ignored him.

2. What was the name of Harry's owl?
Hedwig was its name.

3. From what platform did Harry's train to Hogwarts leave?
It left from Platform Nine and Three-Quarters.

4. How did Harry get through to his train platform?
He walked directly at the barrier between Platforms 9 and 10 and just passed through.

5. Who were Percy, Fred, George, and Ron Weasley?
They were four red-haired brothers Harry met at the train station.

6. Who did Harry meet for a second time at the train station?
He met Draco Malfoy.

7. Why did everyone at the train station stare at and want to meet Harry?
He was famous, and they had already heard of him.

Key - Study Questions - **Harry Potter** - page 6

8. What were Bertie Bott's Every Flavor Beans?
   They were beans of literally **every** flavor.

9. Why didn't Ron buy anything to eat on the train?
   He didn't buy anything because he couldn't afford to.

10. What came inside the Chocolate Frogs that Harry bought?
    Cards for collecting and trading came in them.

11. What girl did Harry meet on the train?
    He met Hermione Granger.

12. Who lost and then found his toad on the train?
    Neville Longbottom did.

Chapter Seven
1. Who was the tall, black-haired witch in emerald-green robes who met Hagrid and the first-year students at the door of Hogwarts?
   It was Professor McGonagall.

2. What were the names of the four houses at Hogwarts?
   They were Gryffindor, Hufflepuff, Ravenclaw, and Slytherin.

3. What was the purpose of the Sorting Ceremony?
   Its purpose was to assign first-year students to their houses at Hogwarts.

4. Which house did the Hat choose for Harry?
   The Hat chose Gryffindor for Harry.

5. What were the four words Professor Dumbledore spoke before the banquet at Hogwarts?
   He said, "Nitwit! Blubber! Oddment! Tweak!"

6. What was the real name of the ghost called "Nearly Headless Nick"?
   The ghost's real name was Sir Nicholas de Mimsy.

7. What was the name of the Slytherin ghost?
   Slytherin ghost's name was The Bloody Baron.

Key - Study Questions - **Harry Potter** - page 7

8. What part of the Hogwarts grounds were forbidden to students?
   Students were forbidden to enter the forest.

9. Who was the Hogwarts caretaker?
   The caretaker was Mr. Filch.

10. What area inside of Hogwarts was out of bounds to everyone?
    The third-floor corridor on the right-hand side was out of bounds to everyone.

Chapter Eight
1. Who was the Potions Master at Hogwarts?
   Professor Severus Snape was the Potions Master.

2. How many staircases were there at Hogwarts?
   There were a hundred and forty-two staircases.

3. Who was always tricking first-year students at Gryffindor?
   Peeves the Poltergeist tricked them.

4. What was the name of Filch's cat?
   Filch's cat was named Mrs. Norris.

5. What did the cat do?
   The cat patrolled the corridors alone and alerted Filch to any rule infractions.

6. Who was the dumpy little witch who taught Herbology?
   She was Professor Sprout.

7. Who was Professor Flitwick?
   He was the Charms teacher.

8. What course did Professor Quirrell teach?
   Prof. Quirrell taught Defense Against the Dark Arts.

9. Who invited Harry to come to visit for a cup of tea?
   Hagrid invited him.

10. Which professor picked on Harry in class?
    Professor Snape did.

Key - Study Questions - **Harry Potter** - page 8

11. Who was Fang?
    Fang was Hagrid's enormous black boarhound.

12. What interesting news was found in the **Daily Prophet**?
    There was news of a break-in at Gringotts.

Chapter Nine

1. What was the only class that Gryffindors and Slytherins took together?
   They took Flying Class together.

2. What gift did Neville's grandmother send to him?
   She sent him a Remembrall.

3. Who was the teacher for flying lessons?
   Madame Hooch was.

4. What happened to Neville when he first flew?
   He fell off his broomstick and landed face down on the grass.

5. How did Harry get chosen for the Quidditch team?
   Professor McGonagall recommended him after seeing him flying for the first time on his broomstick.

6. Who was Oliver Wood?
   Oliver Wood was the captain of the Gryffindor Quidditch team.

7. What was the password to get past the portrait of the fat lady?
   "Pig snout" was the password.

8. Who challenged Harry to a duel?
   Draco Malfoy challenged him.

9. How was Harry tricked about the duel?
   Malfoy tipped off Filch that Harry and Ron would be in the trophy room.

10. What creature frightened Harry and his friends in the forbidden third-floor corridor?
    Fluffy, the three-headed guard dog frightened them.

Key - Study Questions - **Harry Potter** - page 9

Chapter Ten

1. What was in the long, thin package sent to Harry in the Great Hall?
   A new Nimbus Two Thousand brook stick was in the package.

2. How many players were on a Quidditch team?
   Seven players made a team.

3. What was the Quidditch ball called?
   The ball was called the Quaffle.

4. What was Harry's position on the Quidditch team?
   He was the Seeker.

5. When was a Quidditch match over?
   The match was over when a Seeker caught the Golden Snitch.

6. How many points were awarded for catching the Golden Snitch?
   One hundred and fifty points were awarded.

7. Why didn't Harry and Ron return to their dormitory when they heard about the troll?
   They went looking for Hermione.

8. In what room did Harry and Ron lock the troll?
   They locked it in the girls' bathroom.

9. What were the words of the spell that Ron used on the troll?
   Wingardium Leviosa!

10. Who took the blame when Professor McGonagall found that Ron, Harry, and Hermione were not in their dormitory?
    Hermione took the blame.

Chapter Eleven

1. What book about Quidditch did Hermione lend to Harry?
   Hermione let him borrow **Quidditch Through the Ages**.

2. What did Harry see happening between Snape and Filch?
   He saw them examining Snape's leg where he had been bitten by the guard dog.

Key - Study Questions - **Harry Potter** - page 10

3. What did Hermione do to Snape when she thought he was putting a spell on Harry's broomstick?
   She temporarily set him on fire.

4. How did Harry win the Quidditch game for the Gryffindors?
   He caught the Golden Snitch in his mouth.

5. What was the score of the game that Gryffindor won against Slytherin?
   One hundred and seventy to sixty was the score.

6. What name did Hagrid inadvertently give to Harry, Ron, and Hermione?
   Nicolas Flamel

<u>Chapter Twelve</u>

1. As Christmas approached, how was Malfoy taunting Harry?
   He taunted him about not having a proper family.

2. How did Ron, Harry, and Hermione try to find out about Nicolas Flamel?
   They searched through books in the library.

3. What was the name of the librarian at Hogwarts?
   Madam Pince was the librarian.

4. How was wizard chess different from regular chess?
   In wizard chess, the figures were alive.

5. What Christmas gifts did Harry receive?
   He received a wooden flute, a fifty-pence note, a Weasley sweater, a large box of Chocolate Frogs, and an invisibility cloak

6. How did Harry decide to test the invisibility cloak?
   He decided to test it by using it to get in and out of the Restricted Section of the library.

7. What did Harry see in the Mirror of Erised?
   He saw his family.

8. What did Professor Dumbledore say the mirror showed people?
   He said it showed them nothing more or less than the deepest, most desperate desire of their hearts.

Key - Study Questions - **Harry Potter** - page 11

Chapter Thirteen

1. Who was the referee for the home championship Quidditch game?
   Snape was the referee.

2. What curse was put on Neville by Malfoy?
   Malfoy put a leg-locker curse on Neville.

3. How did Harry finally remember having read something about Flamel?
   He saw another Dumbledore collecting card that mentioned Flamel.

4. What was said about Flamel in Hermione's book?
   It said that he was the *only known maker of the Sorcerer's Stone*.

5. What was the Sorcerer's Stone said to be able to do?
   It was said to be able to make gold and to make people immortal.

6. What did Malfoy constantly taunt Ron about?
   He taunted him about being poor.

7. How did the championship Quidditch game end?
   Harry caught the Golden Snitch.

8. How long did the championship Quidditch game last?
   It lasted five minutes.

9. What interaction did Harry think he had witnessed between Snape and Quirrell?
   He thought he witnessed Snape forcing Quirrell to help him to get the Sorcerer's Stone.

10. Why was Harry not interested in the victory party in the Gryffindor common room?
    He was too eager to share with Ron and Hermione what he had witnessed between Snape and Quirrell in the forbidden forest

Chapter Fourteen

1. What did Hermione keep nagging Ron and Harry to do?
   Hermione nagged them to study for their exams.

2. What was Hagrid looking up in the library?
   He was looking up information about dragons.

Key - Study Questions - **Harry Potter** - page 12

3. What was Hagrid keeping illegally in his hut?
   Hagrid kept a dragon egg, and then a dragon

4. Who knew how to get past Fluffy?
   Only Dumbledore and Hagrid knew.

5. What was in the huge black egg in the middle of the fire in Hagrid's hut?
   It was a Norwegian Ridgeback dragon.

6. Who looked in the window and saw the dragon at Hagrid's?
   Malfoy looked in.

7. What was the dragon's name?
   Its name was Norbert.

8. How did Ron, Harry, and Hermione get the dragon out of Hogwarts territory?
   Some of Charlie Weasley's friends took it away for Charlie.

Chapter Fifteen

1. What did Professor McGonagall say that lessened somewhat the severity of Harry, Hermione, and Neville's actions?
   She said that Draco Malfoy was told a cock-and-bull story about a dragon just to get him out of bed and that Neville Longbottom heard the story and believed it too.

2. Why did Harry suddenly become one of the most hated students at Hogwarts?
   He lost points for Gryffindor, thus giving the most points to Slytherin

3. What were the students supposed to find in the forest?
   They were supposed to find a hurt unicorn.

4. What were the beasts in the forest who were part man and part horse?
   They were centaurs.

5. How was Harry rescued from the cloaked figure who drank the unicorn's blood?
   He was rescued by a centaur.

6. What was the note that Harry found pinned to the invisibility cloak when it was returned to him?
   The note said, *"Just in case."*

Key - Study Questions - **Harry Potter** - page 13

Chapter Sixteen
1. How were the written exams bewitched?
    They were bewitched with an Anti-Cheating spell.

2. What were the practical exams?
    The students had to make a pineapple tapdance across a desk, turn a mouse into a snuffbox, and make a Forgetfulness potion.

3. Who gave away the secret of how to get past Fluffy?
    Hagrid gave it away.

4. Why did Harry decide to risk going after the Sorcerer's Stone himself?
    He said that if Voldemort managed to come back, there wouldn't even be a Hogwarts, so it wouldn't matter if he, Harry, got expelled.

5. How did Hermione keep Neville from going with her, Ron, and Harry to seek the Stone?
    She put him in the full Body-Bind.

6. How did Harry, Ron, and Hermione get past Peeves?
    Harry pretended to be the Bloody Baron.

7. What immediately put Fluffy to sleep?
    Music did.

8. What did Ron and Harry fall into when they dropped through the trap door?
    They fell into a Devil's Snare.

9. What were the objects that looked like small, jewel-bright birds?
    They were winged keys.

10. What did Ron, Hermione, and Harry have to do to get past the chessboard?
    They had to actually be chessmen themselves.

Chapter Seventeen
1. What was Harry's great revelation about Snape and Quirrell?
    Quirrell, not Snape, was the real enemy.

Key - Study Questions - **Harry Potter** - page 14

2. Who was Quirrell's master?
   Voldemort was Quirrell's master.

3. How did Harry wind up in possession of the Sorcerer's Stone?
   Harry's reflection in the mirror smiled at him, put its hand into its pocket and pulled out a blood-red stone, winked at Harry and put the Stone back in its pocket–and Harry felt the Stone drop into his real pocket.

4. Where did Harry see Voldemort's face revealed?
   He saw it on the back of Quirrell's head, under his turban.

5. How was Quirrell kept from doing a curse on Harry?
   Harry kept Quirrell in contact with Harry's skin, keeping him in constant pain.

6. What ultimately happened to the Sorcerer's Stone?
   It was destroyed.

7. Why was the Sorcerer's Stone ultimately not such a wonderful thing?
   It gave the two things most human beings would choose above all–but humans have a knack for choosing those things that are worst for them

8. How did Harry's mother's love for him protect him against Quirrell?
   Harry's mother's love left a mark on him and it was agony for Quirrell to touch a person marked by something so good.

9. Why had Professor Snape tried to protect Harry?
   He tried to protect Harry because Harry's father had saved Snape's life. Snape thought if he could protect Harry, his debt to Harry's father would be repaid and he could go back to hating him.

10. How had Harry managed to get the Sorcerer's Stone out of the mirror?
    Harry was the only one who wanted to **find** the stone, not use it.

11. What present did Hagrid bring to Harry in the hospital wing?
    Hagrid brought a handsome, leather-covered book from the pages of which Harry's parents smiled and waved at him

Key - Study Questions - **Harry Potter** - page 15

12. How did Gryffindor wind up winning the house cup?
    Professor Dumbledore added house points for Ron's chess game, for Hermione's use of cool logic, for Harry's nerve and courage, and for Neville's bravery in standing up to his friends when he felt he needed to.

13. Which student was most surprised at being awarded points?
    Neville was the most surprised.

14. Why did Harry say that he would actually have a good holiday with the Dursleys?
    Because **they** (the Dursleys) don't know that the Hogwarts students are not allowed to use magic at home.

Study Guide/Quiz Questions - Harry Potter
Multiple Choice Format

<u>Chapter One</u>

1. What did the reader learn about Mr. and Mrs. Dursley in the book's first paragraph?
    a. They were wizards in disguise.
    b. They were "perfectly normal" people.
    c. They were really named Potter.
    d. They were descended from trolls.

2. What did Mr. Dursley do for a living?
    a. He was a big-time politician.
    b. He was a fireman.
    c. He was the director of Grunnings, a firm which made drills.
    d. He was the supervisor of a plastics manufacturing firm.

3. What big secret did Mr. and Mrs. Dursley want to keep?
    a. They wanted to keep their son a secret.
    b. They wanted to keep secret the fact that they were gypsies.
    c. They wanted to keep their embezzlement from the bank a secret.
    d. They wanted to keep Mrs. Dursley's sister a secret.

4. What was the first unusual thing that Mr. Dursley thought he saw as he left for work?
    a. He thought he saw a huge dog chasing its tail.
    b. He thought he saw a storm coming up.
    c. He thought he saw a cat reading a map.
    d. He thought he saw Harry Potter crossing the street ahead of him.

5. What was unusual about the people Mr. Dursley saw while he waited in a traffic jam?
    a. They were muttering about Mrs. Dursley.
    b. The people were strangely dressed in cloaks.
    c. The people were naked.
    d. The people were all over 40 years old.

6. When he went to the baker's at lunchtime, whom did Mr. Dursley think he heard people talking about?
    a. He thought he heard people talking about crime in the streets.
    b. He thought he heard them talking about his son Dudley.
    c. He thought he heard people talking about how hot it was that month.
    d. He thought he heard people talking about the presidential campaign.

Study Questions - MC - **Harry Potter** - page 2

7. What unusual occurrences were mentioned that night on television news?
    a. Owls flying in the daytime and a downpour of shooting stars instead of rain
    b. Cats prowling all over the town
    c. The fact that Harry Potter was coming to live with the Dursleys
    d. The fact that the town needed more rain

8. Who was the cat on Privet Drive **really**?
    a. The cat was **really** Professor Dumbledore.
    b. The cat was **really** Draco Malfoy.
    c. The cat was **really** Harry's father.
    d. The cat was **really** Professor McGonagall..

9. What person suddenly appeared next to the cat?
    a. Draco Malfoy
    b. Dudley Dursley
    c. Hermione Granger
    d. Albus Dumbledore

10. Why was Albus Dumbledore in the Dursleys' neighborhood?
    a. He had heard about the beauty of Privet Drive.
    b. He was doing a survey of the neighborhood.
    c. He had come to ask that Harry become a junior wizard.
    d. He had come to bring Harry Potter to his aunt and uncle.

11. How did Hagrid arrive in the Dursleys' neighborhood?
    a. He dropped out of a large cloud.
    b. He came to spy on Harry's meeting with Voldemort.
    c. He came to meet the Dursley family.
    d. He arrived out of the air on a huge motorcycle.

12. What did Harry Potter's scar look like?
    a. His scar looked like a miniature goblin.
    b. His scar looked like a big birthmark.
    c. His scar looked like a large cat.
    d. His scar looked like a bolt of lightning.

Study Questions - MC - **Harry Potter** - page 3

Chapter Two

1. What dream was Harry having when his aunt woke him in the morning?
    a. He was dreaming about a flying motorcycle.
    b. He was dreaming about his parents.
    c. He was dreaming about becoming a famous wizard.
    d. He was dreaming about winning the lottery.

2. Where in the Dursley house did Harry sleep?
    a. He slept in the largest bedroom.
    b. He slept on a couch in the living room.
    c. He slept in a small shed on the Dursleys' property.
    d. He slept in a cupboard under the stairs.

3. What was the first rule for a quiet life with the Dursleys?
    a. Don't make waves.
    b. Don't ever cry.
    c. Don't ask questions.
    d. Don't sass adults.

4. Who got all of the good things in the Dursley household?
    a. Dudley Dursley, Harry's cousin
    b. Harry's owl
    c. Mrs. Dursley
    d. Harry

5. What was Dudley Dursley's complaint about his birthday presents?
    a. They didn't cost enough money.
    b. They were just like the ones he got the year before.
    c. They were clumsily wrapped.
    d. He didn't get enough of them.

6. Who was Mrs. Figg?
    a. She was Dudley's cat.
    b. She was a favorite neighbor of Harry's.
    c. She was a mad, old lady who lived two streets away from the Dursleys.
    d. She was Harry's elementary school principal.

Study Questions - MC - **Harry Potter** - page 4

7. Why did Harry finally get to go to the zoo with the Dursley family?
   a. Because Dudley asked him to go with them
   b. Because his aunt and uncle weren't able to think of anything else to do with him
   c. Because the family all voted for him to go
   d. Because he had been extremely good all month long

8. What kind of strange things often happened around Harry?
   a. A dog followed him home, and the dog's mother came looking for it.
   b. His hair was cut and grew back overnight; he gained an enormous amount of weight suddenly; and snakes all stopped in the garden to talk with him.
   c. His hair was cut and grows back overnight; his sweater shrank all on its own; and he was able to leap onto a chimney.
   d. Strangers kept following him home.

9. What strange occurrence happened in connection with Harry at the reptile house?
   a.. A snake communicated with him, then the glass front on the snake's tank vanished and the snake was able just to slither away.
   b. Two snakes asked Harry to play chess with them.
   c. One of the biggest snakes danced and sang a song.
   d. One of the smaller snakes asked Harry his name.

10. What strange vision did Harry have about his dead parents?
    a. He saw their faces in a department store window.
    b. He imagined he saw them saving his life.
    c. He saw a blinding flash of green light and had a burning pain on his forehead.
    d. He saw them smiling at the birth of a new baby.

Study Questions - MC - **Harry Potter** - page 5

<u>Chapter Three</u>
1. What was Dudley's favorite sport?
    a. It was soccer.
    b. It was Quidditch.
    c. It was Harry Hunting.
    d. It was basketball.

2. What was the difference in the schools Dudley and Harry were going to attend?
    a. Dudley's school was in town; Harry's school was in the country.
    b. Dudley's school was St. Slytherin's; Harry's was St. Gryffindor's.
    c. Dudley was to attend Smeltings, an old private school; Harry was to attend Stonewall High, the local public school.
    d. Harry's school was in London; Dudley's school was way out in the country.

3. What was the difference in the two boys' school uniforms?
    a. Dudley had a brand new uniform; Harry had some of Dudley's old things dyed gray.
    b. Dudley's were all white and silky; Harry's were made of harsh fabric.
    c. Harry's were black robes; Dudley's were corduroy pants and shirt.
    d. Harry's were very regal looking; Dudley's were commonplace.

4. What was unusual about the mail that arrived at the Dursley residence the day before Harry's eleventh birthday?
    a. A letter arrived addressed to Harry in The Cupboard under the Stairs.
    b. A letter arrived from his friend Hermione Granger.
    c. One of the letters was marked, "Postage Due."
    d. One of the letters was clearly addressed to Dudley Dursley.

5. Why did Mr. and Mrs. Dursley move Harry into a different bedroom?
    a. Because they felt sorry for him
    b. Because they felt guilty about not giving him a bigger room
    c. Because it was clear that someone watching them knew that Harry lived in a cupboard
    d. Because they had promised him a larger room when he was eleven

6. What was in Harry's new bedroom?
    a. All the best furniture in the house
    b. All of Dudley's discarded things and his unread books
    c. Everything Harry had brought with him from his parents' house
    d. All of the wonderful books on wizardry that Harry had collected

Study Questions - MC - **Harry Potter** - page 6

7. What about Harry's second letter convinced Mr. Dursley that someone was watching the family?
    a. The second letter threatened to turn the Dursleys in to the police.
    b. The second letter was addressed to Harry in The Smallest Bedroom.
    c. It mentioned that Mr. and Mrs. Dursley were related to the Potters.
    d. It revealed many small details about the Dursleys' living room.

8. Why did Mr. Dursley nail the mail slot shut?
    a. So that no mail could be delivered
    b. So that the mailman couldn't spy on them
    c. Because it caused too much of a draft in the house
    d. Because it seemed so middle class to him

9. Why did Mr. Dursley make everyone leave the house?
    a. Because the house seemed like it was a fire hazard
    b. Because more and more letters addressed to Harry arrived at the house
    c. Because he thought it would be good for them to travel
    d. Because he needed a change of surroundings

10. What strange thing happened at the hotel?
    a. Everyone stared at Harry.
    b. Mrs. Dursley had too much to drink in the bar.
    c. Hundreds of letters arrived addressed to Harry in Room 17 of the Railview Hotel.
    d. More than thirty letters arrived addressed to The Traveling Dursley Family.

Study Questions - MC - **Harry Potter** - page 7

<u>Chapter Four</u>

1. Who arrived with a BOOM at the little shack?
    a. Professor Dumbledore, Headmaster of Hogwarts
    b. Rubeus Hagrid, Keeper of Keys and Grounds at Hogwarts
    c. George Weasley, First-Year Student at Hogwarts
    d. A twelve-foot troll

2. What letter did Harry receive from Hagrid?
    a. A special letter that was written by Harry's mother just before she died
    b. A wonderful letter from Hermione Granger
    c. A letter of acceptance at Hogwarts School of Witchcraft and Wizardry
    d. A letter from Professor Dumbledore inviting Harry to tour Hogwarts School

3. How did Hagrid communicate with Professor Dumbledore from the shack?
    a. He sent Dumbledore a telegram.
    b. He sent a special message by carrier pigeon.
    c. He asked Mr. Dursley to write to him.
    d. He sent Dumbledore a letter via owl.

4. What were Muggles?
    a. Nonmagic folk
    b. People who lived in the town
    c. Old people
    d. Stupid folk

5. What did Harry learn about himself from Hagrid?
    a. He learned that he was really only nine years old.
    b. He learned that he was really the Dursleys' own son.
    c. He learned that he, Harry, was a wizard.
    d. He learned that he, Harry, was a genius.

6. What did Harry learn about how his parents died?
    a. He learned that his parents died by being blown up, not by being killed in an automobile accident.
    b. He learned that his parents committed suicide.
    c. He learned that his parents were gunned down in their neighborhood.
    d. He learned that his parents were executed by a foreign government.

Study Questions - MC - **Harry Potter** - page 8

7. Who was Voldemort?
    a. He was Mrs. Dursley's grandfather.
    b. He was a troll.
    c. He was descended from a goblin.
    d. He was a wizard gone bad.

8. What caused Harry's scar?
    a. His father hit him one night when he was drinking.
    b. Voldemort caused the scar when he tried to kill Harry.
    c. Harry fell from his bicycle and hit his face on concrete.
    d. Harry was born with the scar.

9. What did Harry remember for the first time about the night his parents died?
    a. He remembered hearing a high, cold, cruel laugh.
    b. He remembered how much his mother cried.
    c. He remembered his father's awful laughter.
    d. He remembered seeing Professor Dumbledore in the house.

10. What magic did Hagrid strike Dudley with?
    a. He gave Dudley a curly pig's tail which stuck right through Dudley's pants.
    b. He put Dudley in a Full-Body Lock.
    c. He made Dudley oink like a baby pig.
    d. He put Dudley under a spell that made him apologize for treating Harry badly.

Study Questions - MC - **Harry Potter** - page 9

Chapter Five

1. How did Hagrid get to the shack in the middle of the water?
    a. He flew there.
    b. He rented a boat on the other shore.
    c. He was rowed across by a friendly goblin.
    d. He walked across the water.

2. What was Gringotts?
    a. Gringotts was a large department store for wizard clothing.
    b. Gringotts was a wizard bank.
    c. Gringotts was a store that sold wizard wands.
    d. Gringotts was a secret pub.

3. Where was Gringotts?
    a. Hundreds of miles from civilization
    b. About thirty miles outside of London
    c. Hundreds of miles under London, deep under the Underground
    d. Nearly fifty miles from the center of London

4. Who ran Gringotts?
    a. It was run by trolls.
    b. It was run by centaurs.
    c. It was run by wizards.
    d. It was run by goblins.

5. How were the high security vaults at Gringotts guarded?
    a. They were guarded by goblins.
    b. They were guarded by Brinks security guards.
    c. They were guarded by specially trained wizards.
    d. They were guarded by German shepherd dogs.

6. What did Hagrid and Harry need to purchase in Diagon Alley?
    a. Special supplies for Hogwarts School (sugar, candies, treats for the trolls, and a special peppermint patty that Professor Dumbledore liked)
    b. School supplies for Harry (uniform, books, a wand, a cauldron, a set of phials, a telescope, a set of brass scales, and–optionally–an owl OR a cat OR a toad)
    c. Sixty dollars worth of candy for a special party to be held that night
    d. A nice suit for Hagrid to wear at a Hogwarts party

Study Questions - MC - **Harry Potter** - page 10

7. What was the name of the pub Hagrid and Harry visited?
   a. The Leaky Faucet
   b. The Big Pub
   c. Whiskey for Wizards
   d. The Leaky Cauldron

8. What was Professor Quirrell's most notable trait?
   a. He stuttered.
   b. He laughed a lot.
   c. He had a nice smile.
   d. He had a beard.

9. What did Hagrid pick up at Gringotts?
   a. Something that was *very* expensive
   b. Something that he wanted to keep for his own
   c. Something referred to as the You-Know-What in vault seven hundred and thirteen
   d. Something he had always wanted to get for his mother

10. What was so unusual about the wand Harry got at Ollivander's?
    a. It had only one tail feather in it.
    b. It was the shortest wand Ollivander's had ever made.
    c. The tail feather in Harry's wand belonged to a phoenix who gave a second tail feather to the wand belonging to Voldemort.
    d. The wand used to belong to Voldemort.

Study Questions - MC - **Harry Potter** - page 11

Chapter Six

1. How did the Dursleys treat Harry when he returned home?
    a. They showered him with kindness.
    b. They tried to make amends for their past ill will.
    c. They were awful toward him.
    d. They mostly ignored him.

2. What was the name of Harry's owl?
    a. Norbert
    b. Hedwig
    c. Scabbers
    d. Hermione

3. From what platform did Harry's train to Hogwarts leave?
    a. It left from Platform Six and One-Half.
    b. It left from Platform Six-O-Three.
    c. It left from Platform Eleven.
    d. It left from Platform Nine and Three-Quarters.

4. How did Harry get through to his train platform?
    a. He walked directly at the barrier between Platforms 9 and 10 and just passed through.
    b. He jumped over two other platforms and then ran for it.
    c. He just imagined himself there.
    d. Hagrid put a spell on him which allowed him to pass through a wall.

5. Who were Percy, Fred, George, and Ron Weasley?
    a. They were four toads that Neville Longbottom brought from home.
    b. They were all prefects at Gryffindor House.
    c. They were four red-haired brothers that Harry met at the train station.
    d. They were all star Quidditch players at the school.

6. Who did Harry meet for a second time at the train station?
    a. Neville Longbottom
    b. Draco Malfoy
    c. Mr. Ollivander
    d. Hagrid

Study Questions - MC - **Harry Potter** - page 12

7. Why did everyone at the train station stare at and want to meet Harry?
    a. Because he was the only boy not dressed in a robe
    b. Because he was famous and they had already heard of him
    c. Because he was one of the shortest boys there
    d. Because he was very good looking and smart

8. What were Bertie Bott's Every Flavor Beans?
    a. They were beans sold in a special broth.
    b. They were beans that changed flavor based on the person eating them.
    c. They were beans of literally **every** flavor.
    d. They were edible Mexican jumping beans.

9. Why didn't Ron buy anything to eat on the train?
    a. He knew the food was really bad.
    b. He wasn't a bit hungry.
    c. He hated train food.
    d. He didn't buy anything because he couldn't afford to.

10. What came inside the Chocolate Frogs that Harry bought?
    a. Caramel nougats
    b. Peppermint treats
    c. Cards for collecting and trading
    d. Advertisements for wizard training

11. What girl did Harry meet on the train?
    a. Petunia Dursley
    b. Hermione Granger
    c. Hagrid's sister
    d. Susan Bones

12. Who lost and then found his toad on the train?
    a. Ron Weasley
    b. Draco Malfoy
    c. Neville Longbottom
    d. Severus Snape

Study Questions - MC - **Harry Potter** - page 13

Chapter Seven

1. Who was the tall, black-haired witch in emerald-green robes who met Hagrid and the first-year students at the door of Hogwarts?
    a. It was Professor Dumbledore.
    b. It was Peeves.
    c. It was Mrs. Norris.
    d. It was Professor McGonagall.

2. What were the names of the four houses at Hogwarts?
    a. Dopey, Sneezy, Harry, and Griffin
    b. Gryffindor, Hufflepuff, Ravenclaw, and Slytherin
    c. Slytherin, Ravenclaw, HuffandPuff, and Nod
    d. Hermione, Ron, George, and Fred

3. What was the purpose of the Sorting Ceremony?
    a. Its purpose was to assign first-year students to their houses at Hogwarts.
    b. Its purpose was to teach the students to deal cards.
    c. Its purpose was to teach students to sort letters that came in the mail.
    d. Its purpose was to scare students when they first arrived at the school.

4. Which house did the Hat choose for Harry?
    a. Slytherin
    b. Toad House
    c. Courage Hall
    d. Gryffindor

5. What were the four words Professor Dumbledore spoke before the banquet at Hogwarts?
    a. Courage, loyalty, fidelity, and strength
    b. Nitwit! Blubber! Oddment! Tweak!
    c. Onward! Upward! Forward! Scoring!
    d. Quidditch, Scores, Snitching, Seeking

6. What was the real name of the ghost called "Nearly Headless Nick"?
    a. The ghost's real name was His Honor, Sir Nick.
    b. His real name was Mr. Saint Nicolas.
    c. The ghost's real name was Sir Nicholas de Mimsy.
    d. The ghost's real name was Nicolas Flamel.

Study Questions - MC - **Harry Potter** - page 14

7. What was the name of the Slytherin ghost?
   a. The Bleeding Heart
   b. The Heartbroken Hamlet
   c. The Bloody Baron
   d. Sir Bloodless Baron

8. What part of the Hogwarts grounds were forbidden to students?
   a. They were forbidden to play near the rose gardens.
   b. They were forbidden to enter the forest.
   c. They were forbidden to enter the corn maize.
   d. They were forbidden to sit in the gardens.

9. Who was the Hogwarts caretaker?
   a. Hagrid
   b. Mr. Filch
   c. Mrs. Norris
   d. Albus Dumbledore

10. What area inside of Hogwarts was out of bounds to everyone?
    a. Professor Dumbledore's room
    b. The coffee shop
    c. The third-floor corridor on the right-hand side
    d. The little room on the fourth floor

Study Questions - MC - **Harry Potter** - page 15

<u>Chapter Eight</u>
1. Who was the Potions Master at Hogwarts?
   a. Professor Sprout
   b. Mrs. Norris Spencer
   c. Hedwig Owlingown
   d. Professor Severus Snape

2. How many staircases were there at Hogwarts?
   a. There were two thousand staircases.
   b. There were a hundred and forty-two staircases.
   c. There was sixteen hundred twenty-nine staircases.
   d. There were two main staircases and four secondary ones.

3. Who was always tricking first-year students at Gryffindor?
   a. Mrs. Norris
   b. Professor Flitwick
   c. Peeves the Poltergeist
   d. Professor Quirrell

4. What was the name of Filch's cat?
   a. Norbert Ridgeback
   b. Ronnie Weasel
   c. Mrs. Norris
   d. Mr. Fang

5. What did the cat do?
   a. The cat laid around all day doing nothing.
   b. The cat patrolled the corridors alone and alerted Filch to any rule infractions.
   c. The cat looked for food.
   d. The cat hissed at all first-year students.

6. Who was the dumpy little witch who taught Herbology?
   a. Professor Flitwick
   b. Professor Norbert
   c. Professor Scabbers
   d. Professor Sprout

Study Questions - MC - **Harry Potter** - page 16

7. Who was Professor Flitwick?
    a. He was the Flying instructor.
    b. He was the Charms teacher.
    c. He was a former wizard.
    d. He was the brother of Professor Sprout.

8. What course did Professor Quirrell teach?
    a. Making Magic on Mondays
    b. Defense Against the Dark Arts
    c. Herbs for a Happy Haunting
    d. Magic: Ill Will or Good Will?

9. Who invited Harry to come to visit for a cup of tea?
    a. Professor McGonagall invited him.
    b. Hagrid invited him.
    c. Professor Dumbledore invited him.
    d. Hermione invited him.

10. Which professor picked on Harry in class?
    a. Snape
    b. Sprout
    c. Weasley
    d. Norris

11. Who was Fang?
    a. Fang was Professor Dumbledore's collie.
    b. Fang was Hagrid's enormous black boarhound.
    c. Fang was Professor McGonagall's guard dog.
    d. Fang was a facetious name for Mr. Filch's cat.

12. What interesting news was found in the **Daily Prophet**?
    a. News of crimes in London
    b. News of a break-in at Gringotts
    c. News of Professor Flitwick's disappearance.
    d. News of a new movie opening in town

Study Questions - MC - **Harry Potter** - page 17

Chapter Nine

1. What was the only class that Gryffindors and Slytherins took together?
   a. Potions
   b. Flying class
   c. Broomstick mending
   d. Quidditch training

2. What gift did Neville's grandmother send to him?
   a. She sent him a second toad.
   b. She sent him a box of cookies.
   c. She sent him a Remembrall.
   d. She sent him a new sweater.

3. Who was the teacher for flying lessons?
   a. Madame Hooch
   b. Madame Norris
   c. Professor McGonagall
   d. Professor Flitwick

4. What happened to Neville when he first flew?
   a. He fell off his broomstick and landed face down on the grass.
   b. He flew right over the tallest tree around.
   c. He almost fell off his broomstick.
   d. He ran into a tree.

5. How did Harry get chosen for the Quidditch team?
   a. They needed someone of his height.
   b. The players liked his sense of fair play.
   c. He was one of the youngest students at the school.
   d. Professor McGonagall recommended him after seeing him flying for the first time on his broomstick.

6. Who was Oliver Wood?
   a. Oliver Wood was the captain of the Gryffindor Quidditch team.
   b. He was Professor Flitwick's younger brother.
   c. He was one of Hogwarts' youngest graduates.
   d. Oliver Wood was one of Professor Dumbledore's sons.

Study Questions - MC - **Harry Potter** - page 18

7. What was the password to get past the portrait of the fat lady?
    a. "Pretty Lady"
    b. "Pig snout"
    c. "Pretty Please"
    d. "Open Door Please"

8. Who challenged Harry to a duel?
    a. Hagrid
    b. Draco Malfoy
    c. George Weasley
    d. Mr. Filch

9. How was Harry tricked about the duel?
    a. Malfoy tipped off Filch that Harry and Ron would be in the trophy room.
    b. All of the professors knew it was going to take place.
    c. Professor Dumbledore turned him in to Filch.
    d. Someone arranged for Fang to be there when the duel took place.

10. What creature frightened Harry and his friends in the forbidden third-floor corridor?
    a. Scabbers, the rat
    b. Fluffy, the three-headed guard dog
    c. Mrs. Norris, the cat
    d. Norbert the Ridgeback

Study Questions - MC - **Harry Potter** - page 19

<u>Chapter Ten</u>

1. What was in the long, thin package sent to Harry in the Great Hall?
    a. A pogo stick
    b. A shotgun
    c. A new Nimbus Two Thousand broomstick
    d. A broomstick once used by his father

2. How many players were on a Quidditch team?
    a. Seven
    b. Fourteen
    c. Three
    d. Twenty-six

3. What was the Quidditch ball called?
    a. Charlie
    b. Scabbers
    c. The Quaffle
    d. Benji

4. What was Harry's position on the Quidditch team?
    a. He was a Chaser.
    b. He was a Goalie.
    c. He was the Seeker.
    d. He was the Catcher.

5. When was a Quidditch match over?
    a. The match was over when everyone was too tired to play.
    b. The match was over when a team scored two goals in a row.
    c. The match was over when the Seeker fell off his broomstick.
    d. The match was over when a Seeker caught the Golden Snitch.

6. How many points were awarded for catching the Golden Snitch?
    a. Two thousand
    b. Eleven
    c. One hundred and fifty
    d. Three

Study Questions - MC - **Harry Potter** - page 20

7. Why didn't Harry and Ron return to their dormitory when they heard about the troll?
    a. Because they were looking for high adventure
    b. Because they went looking for Hermione
    c. Because they didn't hear the announcement correctly
    d. Because they were both dumb

8. In what room did Harry and Ron lock the troll?
    a. They locked it in Professor Dumbledore's study.
    b. They locked it in Professor Snape's office.
    c. They locked it in a broom closet.
    d. They locked it in the girls' bathroom.

9. What were the words of the spell that Ron used on the troll?
    a. *Lockimus Trollimus!*
    b. *Wingardium Leviosa!*
    c. *Watchium Outus!*
    d. *Trollium Evictus!*

10. Who took the blame when Professor McGonagall found that Ron, Harry, and Hermione were not in their dormitory?
    a. Ron took the blame.
    b. Professor McGonagall took the blame.
    c. Harry took the blame.
    d. Hermione took the blame.

Study Questions - MC - **Harry Potter** - page 21

Chapter Eleven

1. What book about Quidditch did Hermione lend to Harry?
    a. **Seekers Beware!**
    b. **Quidditch is my Life**
    c. **Playing for Keeps**
    d. **Quidditch Through the Ages**

2. What did Harry see happening between Snape and Filch?
    a. He saw them examining a small, well-wrapped package.
    b. He saw them standing over a wounded unicorn.
    c. He saw them examining Snape's leg where he had been bitten by the guard dog.
    d. He saw them counting a great pile of money.

3. What did Hermione do to Snape when she thought he was putting a spell on Harry's broomstick?
    a. She temporarily set him on fire.
    b. She put a Whole-Body curse on him.
    c. She told Dumbledore what was going on.
    d. She screamed.

4. How did Harry win the Quidditch game for the Gryffindors?
    a. He caught the Golden Snitch in his mouth.
    b. He threw an opposing player off his broomstick.
    c. He pretended to be injured.
    d. He injured the opposing Seeker.

5. What was the score of the game that Gryffindor won against Slytherin?
    a. Two to one
    b. Sixty to fifty-nine
    c. One hundred and seventy to sixty
    d. Seven to six

6. What name did Hagrid inadvertently give to Harry, Ron, and Hermione?
    a. James Gryffindor
    b. Nicolas Flamel
    c. Vernon Dursley
    d. Lily Potter

Study Questions - MC - **Harry Potter** - page 22

Chapter Twelve

1. As Christmas approached, how was Malfoy taunting Harry?
    a. He taunted him about not being a good Quidditch player.
    b. He taunted him about his parents being dead.
    c. He taunted him about being friends with Hagrid.
    d. He taunted him about not having a proper family.

2. How did Ron, Harry, and Hermione try to find out about Nicolas Flamel?
    a. They went into London looking for him.
    b. They asked all of their professors about him.
    c. They asked Ron's parents for help.
    d. They searched through books in the library.

3. What was the name of the librarian at Hogwarts?
    a. Madeline Bookworm
    b. Madame Pince
    c. Mrs. Norris
    d. Madame Malfoy

4. How was wizard chess different from regular chess?
    a. In wizard chess, there were no white figures.
    b. In wizard chess, the rules were all different.
    c. In wizard chess, the figures were alive.
    d. There were no significant differences.

5. What Christmas gifts did Harry receive?
    a. A new Nimbus Two Thousand broomstick, a cell phone, two hundred dollars, a huge box of Chocolate Frogs, and a new sweater
    b. A special wand that had been his father's and a broomstick donated by a wealthy alumnus
    c. A wooden flute, a fifty-pence note, a Weasley sweater, a large box of Chocolate Frogs, and an invisibility cloak
    d. An invisibility cloak, a new cauldron, and a baseball cap with Nicolas Flamel's picture on it

Study Questions - MC - **Harry Potter** - page 23

6. How did Harry decide to test the invisibility cloak?
   a. By using it to win at Quidditch
   b. By wearing it to dinner
   c. By using it to get in and out of the Restricted Section of the library
   d. By allowing Hermione to wear it and go into the boys' bathroom

7. What did Harry see in the Mirror of Erised?
   a. Himself excelling at Quidditch
   b. Nicolas Flamel
   c. His family
   d. Ron's whole family

8. What did Professor Dumbledore say the mirror showed people?
   a. He said it showed them how they really looked to others.
   b. He said it showed their inner hearts.
   c. He said it showed them nothing but their true reflection.
   d. He said it showed them nothing more or less than the deepest, most desperate desire of their hearts.

Study Questions - MC - **Harry Potter** - page 24

Chapter Thirteen

1. Who was the referee for the home championship Quidditch game?
    a. Hagrid
    b. Malfoy
    c. Snape
    d. Dumbledore

2. What curse was put on Neville by Malfoy?
    a. A leg-locker curse
    b. A whole-body strangulation
    c. A loser's spell
    d. A troll's delight

3. How did Harry finally remember having read something about Flamel?
    a. He finally found his name in a book in the library.
    b. He saw another Dumbledore collecting card that mentioned Flamel.
    c. He found Flamel's name in the London phone book.
    d. He found Flamel's name on an alumni trophy.

4. What was said about Flamel in Hermione's book?
    a. It said that he was a famous Hogwarts alumnus.
    b. It said that he was a very evil wizard.
    c. It said he had chosen the Hogwarts name for the school.
    d. It said that he was the only known maker of the Sorcerer's Stone.

5. What was the Sorcerer's Stone said to be able to do?
    a. It was said to make everyone fall in love and be happy.
    b. It was said to make everyone who touched it invisible for a day.
    c. It was said to make all who touched it eternally happy.
    d. It was said to make gold and to make people immortal.

6. What did Malfoy constantly taunt Ron about?
    a. He taunted him about his talkative mother.
    b. He taunted him about his prefect brother.
    c. He taunted him about being poor.
    d. He taunted him about his friendship with Harry.

Study Questions - MC - **Harry Potter** - page 25

7. How did the championship Quidditch game end?
   a. Harry fell off his broomstick.
   b. Malfoy called the game off.
   c. Snape disqualified the Gryffindor team.
   d. Harry caught the Golden Snitch.

8. How long did the championship Quidditch game last?
   a. Two months
   b. All day
   c. Sixteen hours
   d. Five minutes

9. What interaction did Harry think he had witnessed between Snape and Quirrell?
   a. Snape forcing Quirrell to help him to get the Sorcerer's Stone
   b. Snape forcing Quirrell to give him a lot of money
   c. Quirrell asking Snape for help in hurting Harry
   d. Quirrell and Snape plotting to kill Dumbledore

10. Why was Harry not interested in the victory party in the Gryffindor common room?
    a. Because the food at Gryffindor parties was always mediocre
    b. Because he was full from the food at the other parties
    c. Because he was too eager to share with Ron and Hermione what he had witnesses between Snape and Quirrell in the forbidden forest
    d. Because Snape had warned him that some of the party food was poisonous

Study Questions - MC - **Harry Potter** - page 26

Chapter Fourteen

1. What did Hermione keep nagging Ron and Harry to do?
    a. To find the Sorcerer's Stone
    b. To appreciate Professor Snape's teaching abilities
    c. To study for their exams
    d. To try to break the Anti-Cheating spell

2. What was Hagrid looking up in the library?
    a. He was looking up information requested by Dumbledore.
    b. He was looking at books about giants.
    c. He was looking for a book about Nicolas Flamel.
    d. He was looking up information about dragons.

3. What was Hagrid keeping illegally in his hut?
    a. A book on ancient spells
    b. A dragon egg, and then a dragon
    c. A friendly goblin
    d. A map of the whole Hogwarts property

4. Who knew how to get past Fluffy?
    a. Harry's parents
    b. Only Nicolas Flamel
    c. Mr. Filch
    d. Only Dumbledore and Hagrid

5. What was in the huge black egg in the middle of the fire in Hagrid's hut?
    a. A chicken
    b. A Hogwarts ostrich
    c. A Norwegian Ridgeback dragon
    d. Three purple chickens

6. Who looked in the window and saw the dragon at Hagrid's?
    a. Mr. Filch
    b. Malfoy
    c. Neville
    d. Ron

Study Questions - MC - **Harry Potter** - page 27

7. What was the dragon's name?
   a. Its name was Drago.
   b. Its name was Hedwig.
   c. Its name was Norbert.
   d. It's name was Albus.

8. How did Ron, Harry, and Hermione get the dragon out of Hogwarts territory?
   a. Neville Longbottom lured it into the forest.
   b. Charlie Weasley came to Hogwarts and picked it up.
   c. Nicolas Flamel took it to his house.
   d. Some of Charlie Weasley's friends took it away for Charlie.

Chapter Fifteen

1. What did Professor McGonagall say that lessened somewhat the severity of Harry, Hermione, and Neville's actions?
   a. She said that Draco Malfoy was a bad boy and that Harry was too good to have gotten in so much trouble.
   b. She said that Draco Malfoy was told a cock-and-bull story about a dragon just to get him out of bed and that Neville Longbottom heard the story and believed it too.
   c. She said that not one of the three of them was smart enough to pull off such a prank.
   d. She said that she could not possibly believe that anyone related to James Potter would have participated in a school prank.

2. Why did Harry suddenly become one of the most hated students at Hogwarts?
   a. Because everybody thought he became snobby when he won at Quidditch
   b. Because he lost points for Gryffindor, thus giving the most points to Slytherin
   c. Because they found out that he had been raised by Muggles
   d. Because he was just too successful for their comfort

3. What were the students supposed to find in the forest?
   a. A centaur
   b. A goblin
   c. A wounded deer
   d. A hurt unicorn

4. What were the beasts in the forest who were part man and part horse?
   a. They were an odd species of goblin.
   b. They were hobgoblins.
   c. They were centaurs.
   d. They were Halloween monsters.

5. How was Harry rescued from the cloaked figure who drank the unicorn's blood?
   a. He was rescued by a friendly troll.
   b. Hermione put a deadly curse on the cloaked figure.
   c. He was rescued by a centaur.
   d. He was rescued by Hagrid.

Study Questions - MC - **Harry Potter** - page 29

6. What was the note that Harry found pinned to the invisibility cloak when it was returned to him?
    a. The note said, *"Wear this tonight."*
    b. The note said, *"Think of me when you wear this cloak."*
    c. The note said, *"Beware of Mrs. Norris."*
    d. The note said, *"Just in case."*

Study Questions - MC - **Harry Potter** - page 30

Chapter Sixteen

1. How were the written exams bewitched?
    a. They were bewitched with an Anti-Cheating spell.
    b. They were written in invisible ink.
    c. The correct answers were all expressed in numeric form.
    d. They were bewitched with an Anti-Correctness curse.

2. What were the practical exams?
    a. The students had to make a professor disappear, catch a mouse in the forest, and put a pig's tail on one of their fellow students.
    b. The students had to do something totally out of character for themselves.
    c. The students had to make a pineapple tapdance across a desk, turn a mouse into a snuffbox, and make a Forgetfulness potion.
    d. The students had to fly higher than they ever had and to make a Happiness potion.

3. Who gave away the secret of how to get past Fluffy?
    a. Hermione
    b. Nicolas Flamel
    c. Snape
    d. Hagrid

4. Why did Harry decide to risk going after the Sorcerer's Stone himself?
    a. He said he had always wanted to be a hero.
    b. He said that his success would make Dudley Dursley know how heroic Harry really was.
    c. He said that if Voldemort managed to come back, there wouldn't even be a Hogwarts, so it wouldn't matter if he, Harry, got expelled.
    d. He said that his parents would expect it of him.

5. How did Hermione keep Neville from going with her, Ron, and Harry to seek the Stone?
    a. She lied to him.
    b. She begged him not to endanger Harry.
    c. She told him the secret of the Stone.
    d. She put him in a full Body-Bind.

Study Questions - MC - **Harry Potter** - page 31

6. How did Harry, Ron, and Hermione get past Peeves?
   a. Harry killed him.
   b. Mrs. Norris put a spell on him.
   c. Harry pretended to be the Bloody Baron.
   d. Hermione charmed him.

7. What immediately put Fluffy to sleep?
   a. Tranquilized dog food
   b. Music
   c. Dog biscuits
   d. A special spell

8. What did Ron and Harry fall into when they dropped through the trap door?
   a. Poison ivy
   b. Nasty Vine
   c. A garland of flowers
   d. Devil's Snare

9. What were the objects that looked like small, jewel-bright birds?
   a. Winged keys
   b. Butterflies
   c. Magic gnats
   d. Live hummingbirds

10. What did Ron, Hermione, and Harry have to do to get past the chessboard?
    a. They had to kill all the chessmen.
    b. They had to put a spell on the white chessmen.
    c. They had to actually be chessmen themselves
    d. They had to read more about chess in an old book.

Study Questions - MC - **Harry Potter** - page 32

Chapter Seventeen

1. What was Harry's great revelation about Snape and Quirrell?
    a. That Snape and Quirrell were actually brothers.
    b. That Quirrell and Snape were actually cousins.
    c. That Quirrell, not Snape, was the real enemy.
    d. That neither Snape nor Quirrell was an enemy.

2. Who was Quirrell's master?
    a. Hagrid
    b. Voldemort
    c. Dumbledore
    d. Mrs. Norris

3. How did Harry wind up in possession of the Sorcerer's Stone?
    a. Harry's reflection in the mirror smiled at him, put its hand into its pocket and pulled out a blood-red stone, winked at Harry and put the Stone back in its pocket–and Harry felt the Stone drop into his real pocket.
    b. One minute the Stone was nowhere to be found and the next it was somehow in Harry's mouth.
    c. Harry wrestled it away from Quirrell.
    d. Ron ran into the room, grabbed the Stone, and tossed it to Harry.

4. Where did Harry see Voldemort's face revealed?
    a. In the Mirror of Erised
    b. On a special collecting card in a Chocolate Frog
    c. On the back of Quirrell's head, under his turban
    d. In his imagination

5. How was Quirrell kept from doing a curse on Harry?
    a. Harry somehow managed to keep far enough away that Quirrell couldn't reach him.
    b. Harry kept Quirrell in contact with Harry's skin, keeping him in constant pain.
    c. Hermione put her curse on Quirrell first.
    d. Hermione set fire to Quirrell's turban.

6. What ultimately happened to the Sorcerer's Stone?
    a. It simply disappeared.
    b. It was destroyed.
    c. It killed Voldemort.
    d. It got lost in all the confusion.

Study Questions - MC - **Harry Potter** - page 33

7. Why was the Sorcerer's Stone ultimately not such a wonderful thing?
    a. Because it was simply too hard to find
    b. Because it gave the two things most human beings would choose above all–but humans have a knack for choosing those things that are worst for them
    c. Because even immortal life doesn't make some people laugh
    d. Because too much money can spoil a person's life

8. How did Harry's mother's love for him protect him against Quirrell?
    a. Because Harry's mother's love gave him inner strength
    b. Because her love made his skin seem like iron
    c. Because Harry's mother's love left a mark on him and it was agony for Quirrell to touch a person marked by something so good
    d. Because a mother's love is special love

9. Why had Professor Snape tried to protect Harry?
    a. He tried to protect Harry because he had always secretly admired him.
    b. He tried to protect Harry because Harry's father had saved Snape's life. Snape thought if he could protect Harry, his debt to Harry's father would be repaid and he could go back to hating him.
    c. Snape wanted to help Harry because Quirrell was so mean to him.
    d. Snape could think of no other way to be a hero at Hogwarts.

10. How had Harry managed to get the Sorcerer's Stone out of the mirror?
    a. Harry was the only one who wanted to **find** the Stone, not use it.
    b. Ron dashed into the room and pulled the Stone through the mirror.
    c. Harry was pure of heart and really wanted the Stone.
    d. Dumbledore willed it so.

11. What present did Hagrid bring to Harry in the hospital wing?
    a. A special leather book about dragons
    b. A dragon's egg
    c. A goblin servant
    d. A handsome, leather-covered book from the pages of which Harry's parents smiled and waved at him

Study Questions - MC - **Harry Potter** - page 34

12. How did Gryffindor wind up winning the house cup?
    a. Professor Dumbledore just decided that the Gryffindors were the most worthy students.
    b. Professor McGonagall gave the Gryffindors extra points because she liked them best.
    c. Professor Dumbledore added house points for Ron's chess game, for Hermione's use of cool logic, for Harry's nerve and courage, and for Neville's bravery in standing up to his friends when he felt he needed to.
    d. The Gryffindors found a magic way to cheat the system.

13. Which student was most surprised at being awarded points?
    a. Hermione
    b. Harry
    c. Neville
    d. Malfoy

14. Why did Harry say that he would actually have a good holiday with the Dursleys?
    a. Because **they** (the Dursleys) are too insignificant to worry about
    b. Because he would be back at Hogwarts soon enough
    c. Because **they** (the Dursleys) don't know that the Hogwarts students are not allowed to use magic at home
    d. Because everybody has a good time at Christmas

Answer Key - Multiple Choice Study/quiz Questions
Harry Potter

Chapter One	Chapter Two	Chapter Three	Chapter Four	Chapter Five	Chapter Six
1. b	1. a	1. c	1. b	1. a	1. d
2. c	2. d	2. c	2. c	2. b	2. b
3. d	3. c	3. a	3. d	3. c	3. d
4. c	4. a	4. a	4. a	4. c	4. a
5. b	5. d	5. c	5. c	5. a	5. c
6. b	6. c	6. b	6. a	6. b	6. b
7. a	7. b	7. b	7. d	7. d	7. b
8. d	8. c	8. a	8. b	8. a	8. c
9. d	9. a	9. b	9. a	9. c	9. d
10. d	10. c	10. c	10. a	10. c	10. c
11. d					11. b
12. d					12. c

Chapter Seven	Chapter Eight	Chapter Nine	Chapter Ten	Chapter Eleven
1. d	1. d	1. b	1. c	1. d
2. b	2. b	2. c	2. a	2. c
3. a	3. c	3. a	3. c	3. a
4. d	4. c	4. a	4. c	4. a
5. b	5. b	5. d	5. d	5. c
6. c	6. d	6. a	6. c	6. b
7. c	7. b	7. b	7. b	
8. b	8. b	8. b	8. d	
9. b	9. b	9. a	9. b	
10. c	10. a	10. b	10. d	
	11. b			
	12. b			

Multiple Choice Study/Quiz Question Answer Key Continued - Harry Potter

Chapter Twelve	Chapter Thirteen	Chapter Fourteen	Chapter Fifteen
1. d	1. c	1. c	1. b
2. d	2. a	2. d	2. b
3. b	3. b	3. b	3. d
4. c	4. d	4. d	4. c
5. c	5. d	5. c	5. c
6. c	6. c	6. b	6. d
7. c	7. d	7. c	
8. d	8. d	8. d	
	9. a		
	10. c		

Chapter Sixteen	Chapter Seventeen
1. a	1. c
2. c	2. b
3. d	3. a
4. c	4. c
5. d	5. b
6. c	6. b
7. b	7. b
8. d	8. c
9. a	9. b
10. c	10. a
	11. d
	12. c
	13. c
	14. c

PRE-READING VOCABULARY WORKSHEETS

Vocabulary - **Harry Potter** Chapter One
Part I: Using Prior Knowledge and Contextual Clues
Below are the sentences in which vocabulary words appear in the text. Read the sentence. Use any clues you can find in the sentence, combined with your prior knowledge, and write what you think the underlined words mean on the lines provided.

1. The Dursleys <u>shuddered</u> to think what the neighbors would say if the Potters arrived in the street.

2. It was on the corner of the street that he noticed the first sign of something <u>peculiar</u>–a cat reading a map.

3. People in <u>cloaks</u>.

4. The cat didn't move. It just gave him a <u>stern</u> look.

5. His blue eyes were light, bright, and sparkling behind half-moon <u>spectacles</u> and his nose was very long and crooked, as though it had been broken at least twice.

6. She looked distinctly <u>ruffled</u>.

7. Professor McGonagall <u>flinched</u>, but Dumbledore, who was unsticking two lemon drops, seemed not to notice.

8. "I'm not saying his heart isn't in the right place," said Professor McGonagall <u>grudgingly</u>, "but you can't pretend he's not careless."

Vocabulary - **Harry Potter** Chapter One, Page 2
Part II: Determining the Meaning

___ 1. shuddered   A. firm, severe
___ 2. peculiar   B. winced
___ 3. cloaks   C. reluctantly
___ 4. stern   D. shivered, as from fear or aversion
___ 5. spectacles   E. disturbed, annoyed
___ 6. ruffled   F. loose outer garments
___ 7. flinched   G. glasses
___ 8. grudgingly   H. odd, unusual

Vocabulary - **Harry Potter** Chapter Two
Part I: Using Prior Knowledge and Contextual Clues
Below are the sentences in which vocabulary words appear in the text. Read the sentence. Use any clues you can find in the sentence, combined with your prior knowledge, and write what you think the underlined words mean on the lines provided.

1. The sun rose on the same tidy front gardens and lit up the brass number four on the Dursleys' front door....

2. Harry, who could see a huge Dudley tantrum coming on, began wolfing down his bacon as fast as possible in case Dudley turned the table over.

3. "Now what?" said Aunt Petunia, looking furiously at Harry as though he'd planned this.

4. Dudley and Piers sniggered.

5. Behind the glass, all sorts of lizards and snakes were crawling and slithering over bits of wood and stone.

6. Dudley stood with his nose pressed against the glass, staring at the glistening brown coils.

7. His aunt and uncle never spoke about them, and of course he was forbidden to ask questions.

Part II: Determining the Meaning

___ 9. tidy   A. angrily
___ 10. tantrum   B. not allowed
___ 11. furiously   C. neat
___ 12. sniggered   D. glittering
___ 13. slithered   E. fit
___ 14. glistening   F. slide, glide
___ 15. forbidden   G. snickered

Vocabulary - **Harry Potter** Chapter Three
Part I: Using Prior Knowledge and Contextual Clues
Below are the sentences in which vocabulary words appear in the text. Read the sentence. Use any clues you can find in the sentence, combined with your prior knowledge, and write what you think the underlined words mean on the lines provided.

1. Smeltings' boys wore maroon tailcoats, orange knickerbockers, and flat straw hats called boaters.

2. As he looked at Dudley in his new knickerbockers, Uncle Vernon said gruffly that it was the proudest moment of his life.

3. He'd screamed, whacked his father with his Smelting stick, been sick on purpose, kicked his mother, and thrown his tortoise through the greenhouse roof, and he still didn't have his room back.

4. "Who on earth wants to talk to *you* this badly?" Dudley asked Harry in amazement.

5. Next moment, thirty or forty letters came pelting out of the fireplace like bullets.

6. "That does it," said Uncle Vernon, trying to speak calmly but pulling great tufts out of his mustache at the same time.

7. "Wouldn't it be better just to go home, dear?" Aunt Petunia suggested timidly, hours later, but Uncle Vernon didn't seem to hear her.

Part II: Determining the Meaning
___16. knickerbockers   A. hurling
___17. gruffly   B. short strands of hair
___18. whacked   C. wonder
___19. amazement   D. hesitantly
___20. pelting   E. harshly
___21. tufts   F. full pants, gathered below the knee
___22. timidly   G. struck

Vocabulary - **Harry Potter** Chapter Four
Part I: Using Prior Knowledge and Contextual Clues
Below are the sentences in which vocabulary words appear in the text. Read the sentence. Use any clues you can find in the sentence, combined with your prior knowledge, and write what you think the underlined words mean on the lines provided.

1. Harry looked into the fierce, wild, shadowy face and saw that the beetle eyes were crinkled in a smile.
   _____

2. Uncle Vernon made another funny noise, like a mouse being trodden on.
   _____

3. He held out an enormous hand and shook Harry's whole arm.
   _____

4. The Dursleys were cowering against the wall.
   _____

5. A braver man than Vernon Dursley would have quailed under the furious look Hagrid now gave him; when Hagrid spoke, his every syllable trembled with rage.
   _____

6. "Ah, go boil yer heads, both of yes," said Hagrid. "Harry–yer a wizard."
   _____

7. "Why were you expelled?"
   _____

Part II: Determining the Meaning
___23. crinkled   A. very big
___24. trodden   B. magician
___25. enormous   C. forced, put out
___26. cowering   D. wrinkled
___27. quailed   E. walked on
___28. wizard   F. cringing
___29. expelled   G. shrank in fear

Vocabulary - **Harry Potter** Chapter Five
Part I: Using Prior Knowledge and Contextual Clues
Below are the sentences in which vocabulary words appear in the text. Read the sentence. Use any clues you can find in the sentence, combined with your prior knowledge, and write what you think the underlined words mean on the lines provided.

1. Harry tried to wave the owl out of the way, but it snapped its beak fiercely at him and carried on savaging the coat.
   _____

2. "Just the one. Gringotts. Run by goblins."
   _____

3. 1 cauldron (pewter, standard size 2)
   _____

4. It was a tiny, grubby-looking pub.
   _____

5. At last, Hagrid managed to make himself heard over the babble.
   _____

6. Vampires? Hags? Harry's head was swimming.
   _____

Part II: Determining the Meaning
___30. savaging   A. witches
___31. goblin   B. foolish talk
___32. cauldron   C. attacking violently
___33. pub   D. grotesque elfin creature
___34. babble   E. large kettle, for boiling
___35. hags   F. tavern, bar

Vocabulary - **Harry Potter** Chapter Six
Part I: Using Prior Knowledge and Contextual Clues
Below are the sentences in which vocabulary words appear in the text. Read the sentence. Use any clues you can find in the sentence, combined with your prior knowledge, and write what you think the underlined words mean on the lines provided.

1. Grunt. Harry supposed that meant yes.

2. "Don't talk rubbish," said Uncle Vernon. "There is no platform nine and three-quarters."

3. Getting desperate, Harry asked for the train that left at eleven o'clock, but the guard said there wasn't one.

4. "Excuse me," Harry said to the plump woman.

5. People jostled him on their way to platforms nine and ten.

6. "You've already seen him, Ginny, and the poor boy isn't something you goggle at in a zoo."

7. For some reason, he was looking gloomy.

8. Then they clambered up a passageway in the rock after Hagrid's lamp, coming out at last onto smooth, damp grass right in the shadow of the castle.

Part II: Determining the Meaning
___36. supposed   A. student officer
___37. rubbish   B. pushed, elbowed
___38. desperate   C. stare
___39. plump   D. climbed with difficulty
___40. jostled   E. dark, dreary
___41. goggle   F. garbage, trash
___42. gloomy   G. nearly hopeless
___43. prefect   H. chubby, full in figure
___44. clambered   I. assumed to be true

Vocabulary - **Harry Potter** Chapter Seven
Part I: Using Prior Knowledge and Contextual Clues
Below are the sentences in which vocabulary words appear in the text. Read the sentence. Use any clues you can find in the sentence, combined with your prior knowledge, and write what you think the underlined words mean on the lines provided.

1. Her eyes lingered for a moment on Neville's cloak, which was fastened under his left ear, and on Ron's smudged nose.
   _____

2. A few people nodded mutely.
   _____

3. "I'll kill Fred, he was going on about wrestling a troll."
   _____

4. "Peeves," Percy whispered to the first years. "A poltergeist."
   _____

5. He was wearing Professor Quirrell's turban, which kept talking to him, telling him he must transfer to Slytherin at once, because it was his destiny.
   _____

Part II: Determining the Meaning

___45. lingered   A. fate
___46. mutely   B. annoyed
___47. troll   C. ghost that announces its presence
___48. craning   D. delayed leaving
___49. miffed   E. stretching, straining
___50. poltergeist   F. silently
___51. destiny   G. supernatural creature

Vocabulary - **Harry Potter** Chapter Eight

Part I: Using Prior Knowledge and Contextual Clues

Below are the sentences in which vocabulary words appear in the text. Read the sentence. Use any clues you can find in the sentence, combined with your prior knowledge, and write what you think the underlined words mean on the lines provided.

1. Hermione Granger was on the edge of her seat and looked desperate to start proving that she wasn't a dunderhead.
   _____

2. Snape's lips curled into a sneer.
   _____

3. A crossbow and a pair of galoshes were outside the front door.
   _____

4. When Harry knocked they heard a frantic scrabbling from inside and several booming barks.
   _____

Part II: Determining the Meaning

___52. dunderhead   A. waterproof overshoes
___53. sneer   B. scraping
___54. galoshes   C. dunce, dummy
___55. scrabbling   D. scornful facial expression

Vocabulary - **Harry Potter** Chapter Nine
Part I: Using Prior Knowledge and Contextual Clues
Below are the sentences in which vocabulary words appear in the text. Read the sentence. Use any clues you can find in the sentence, combined with your prior knowledge, and write what you think the underlined words mean on the lines provided.

1. Malfoy's eagle owl was always bringing him packages of sweets from home, which he opened gloatingly at the Slytherin table.
   _____

2. Hovering level with the topmost branches of an oak he called, "Come and get it, Potter!"
   _____

3. But Wood turned out to be a person, a burly fifth-year boy who came out of Flitwick's class looking confused.
   _____

4. There was of course nothing at all little about Crabb and Gayle, but as the High Table was full of teachers, neither of them could do more than crack their knuckles and scowl.
   _____

5. Harry couldn't believe anyone could be so interfering.
   _____

6. "Oh, move over," Hermione snarled.
   _____

7. "No, *not* the floor. It was standing on a trapdoor. It's obviously guarding something.
   _____

Part II: Determining the Meaning

___56. gloatingly   A. meddling
___57. hovering   B. growled
___58. burly   C. hinged or sliding door
___59. scowl   D. floating suspended in air
___60. interfering   E. husky
___61. snarled   F. in a self-satisfied way
___62. trapdoor   G. frown angrily

Vocabulary - **Harry Potter** Chapter Ten
Part I: Using Prior Knowledge and Contextual Clues
Below are the sentences in which vocabulary words appear in the text. Read the sentence. Use any clues you can find in the sentence, combined with your prior knowledge, and write what you think the underlined words mean on the lines provided.

1. Harry had difficulty hiding his glee as he handed the note to Ron to read.
   _____

2. Malfoy seized the package from Harry and felt it.
   _____

3. Harry swung at it with the bat to stop it from breaking his nose, and sent it zigzagging away into the air...."
   _____

4. On Halloween morning they woke to the delicious smell of baking pumpkin wafting through the corridors.
   _____

5. Flushed with their victory, they started to run back up the passageway, but as they reached the corner they heard something that made their hearts stop–a high, petrified scream–and it was coming from the chamber they'd just chained up.
   _____

Part II: Determining the Meaning

___63. glee   A. moving gently
___64. seized   B. grabbed
___65. zigzagging   C. joy
___66. wafting   D. paralyzed with terror
___67. petrified   E. moving with sharp turns

Vocabulary - **Harry Potter** Chapter Eleven
Part I: Using Prior Knowledge and Contextual Clues
Below are the sentences in which vocabulary words appear in the text. Read the sentence. Use any clues you can find in the sentence, combined with your prior knowledge, and write what you think the underlined words mean on the lines provided.

1. One of his legs was bloody and <u>mangled</u>.

2. Snape's face was twisted with <u>fury</u> as he dropped his robes quickly to hide his leg.

3. "Harry, you need your strength," said Seamus Finnigan. "Seekers are always the ones who get <u>clobbered</u>."

4. Harry's broom had started to roll over and over, with him only just managing to hold on.

Part II: Determining the Meaning

___68. mangled   A. battered
___69. fury   B. hanging loosely
___70. clobbered   C. intense anger, rage
___71. dangling   D. torn, mutilated

Vocabulary - **Harry Potter** Chapter Twelve

Part I: Using Prior Knowledge and Contextual Clues

Below are the sentences in which vocabulary words appear in the text. Read the sentence. Use any clues you can find in the sentence, combined with your prior knowledge, and write what you think the underlined words mean on the lines provided.

1. Hagrid had obviously whittled it himself.
   _____

2. Ron was fascinated by the fifty pence.
   _____

3. Sure enough, his reflection looked back at him, just as his head suspended in midair, his body completely invisible.
   _____

4. "I hate maroon," Ron moaned halfheartedly as he pulled it over his head.
   _____

5. When Harry finally left the table, he was laden down with a stack of things out of the crackers, including a pack of non-explodable, luminous balloons, a Grow-Your-Own-Warts kit, and his own new wizard chess set.
   _____

Part II: Determining the Meaning

___72. whittled   A. burdened
___73. fascinated   B. with little interest
___74. reflection   C. cut, carved
___75. halfheartedly   D. intensely interested
___76. laden   E. image

Vocabulary - **Harry Potter** Chapter Thirteen
Part I: Using Prior Knowledge and Contextual Clues
Below are the sentences in which vocabulary words appear in the text. Read the sentence. Use any clues you can find in the sentence, combined with your prior knowledge, and write what you think the underlined words mean on the lines provided.

1. Harry and Ron barely had time to exchange mystified looks before she was dashing back, an enormous old book in her arms.
   _____

2. It also produces the Elixir of Life, which will make the drinker immortal.
   _____

3. The idea of overtaking Slytherin in the house championship was wonderful, no one had done it for seven years, but would they be allowed to, with such a biased referee?
   _____

4. Quirrell was mumbling something.
   _____

Part II: Determining the Meaning

___77. mystified   A. saying indistinctly
___78. elixir   B. prejudiced
___79. biased   C. bewildered, perplexed
___80. mumbling   D. special medicine

Vocabulary - **Harry Potter** Chapter Fourteen
Part I: Using Prior Knowledge and Contextual Clues
Below are the sentences in which vocabulary words appear in the text. Read the sentence. Use any clues you can find in the sentence, combined with your prior knowledge, and write what you think the underlined words mean on the lines provided.

1. Hagrid shuffled into view, hiding something behind his back.
   _____

2. He looked suddenly suspicious.
   _____

3. He had written only two words: *It's hatching*.
   _____

4. There was a hitch.
   _____

5. Forgetting that they were already invisible, they shrank into the shadows, staring at the dark outlines of two people grappling with each other ten feet away.
   _____

Part II: Determining the Meaning

___81. shuffled   A. struggling
___82. suspicious   B. delay
___83. hatching   C. walked while dragging feet
___84. hitch   D. suspecting
___85. grappling   E. breaking out of an egg

Vocabulary - **Harry Potter** Chapter Fifteen
Part I: Using Prior Knowledge and Contextual Clues
Below are the sentences in which vocabulary words appear in the text. Read the sentence. Use any clues you can find in the sentence, combined with your prior knowledge, and write what you think the underlined words mean on the lines provided.

1. Excuses, alibis, and wild cover-up stories chases each other around Harry's brain, each more feeble than the last.
   _____

2. It's not exactly a secret we hate him, Dumbledore'll think we made it up to get him sacked.
   _____

3. Hermione looked convinced, but Ron didn't.
   _____

4. There were splashes on the roots of a tree, as though the poor creature had been thrashing about in pain close by.
   _____

5. It was the unicorn all right, and it was dead.
   _____

Part II: Determining the Meaning

___86. feeble   A. beating, flailing
___87. sacked   B. fabled horse with horn coming out of head
___88. convinced   C. weak
___89. unicorn   D. fired, let go
___90. thrashing   E. certain

Vocabulary - **Harry Potter** Chapter Sixteen

Chapter Sixteen Part I: Using Prior Knowledge and Contextual Clues

Below are the sentences in which vocabulary words appear in the text. Read the sentence. Use any clues you can find in the sentence, combined with your prior knowledge, and write what you think the underlined words mean on the lines provided.

1. Hagrid suddenly looked horrified.
   _____

2. "I shouldn'ta told yer that!" he blurted out. "Forget I said it! Hey–where're yeh going'?"
   _____

3. "He received an urgent owl from the Ministry of Magic and flew off for London at once."
   _____

4. The books she was carrying tumbled out of her arms, but she didn't pick them up.
   _____

5. Hermione gasped. Harry and Ron wheeled round.
   _____

6. But leaving Neville lying motionless on the floor didn't feel like a very good omen.
   _____

7. A few seconds later, they were there, outside the third-floor corridor–and the door was already ajar.
   _____

8. She had to struggle because the moment she had landed, the plant had started to twist snakelike tendrils around her ankles.
   _____

Part II: Determining the Meaning

___91. horrified   A. stems, shoots
___92. blurted   B. partially open
___93. urgent   C. sign
___94. tumbled   D. very shocked
___95. wheeled   E. said impulsively
___96. omen   F. needing immediate action
___97. ajar   G. fell loosely, haphazardly
___98. tendrils   H. turned suddenly

Vocabulary - **Harry Potter** Chapter Seventeen
Part I: Using Prior Knowledge and Contextual Clues
Below are the sentences in which vocabulary words appear in the text. Read the sentence. Use any clues you can find in the sentence, combined with your prior knowledge, and write what you think the underlined words mean on the lines provided.

1. Quirrell raised his hand to perform a deadly curse, but Harry, by instinct, reached up and grabbed Quirrell's face–

2. "....As much money and life as you could want! The two things most human beings would choose above all–the trouble is, humans do have a knack of choosing precisely those things that are worst for them."

3. "....It was agony to touch a person marked by something so good."

4. Hermione looked ready to fling her arms around him again, but Harry was glad she held herself in as his head was still very sore.

5. "Hagrid!" said Harry, shocked to see Hagrid shaking with grief and remorse, great tears leaking down into his beard.

6. Someone standing outside the Great Hall might well have thought some sort of explosion had taken place, so loud was the noise that erupted from the Gryffindor table.

Part II: Determining the Meaning

____ 99. instinct   A. burst, spewed
____100. knack   B. natural behavior
____101. agony   C. special talent
____102. fling   D. regret
____103. remorse   E. extremely painful
____104. erupted   F. throw

Vocabulary Answer Key - Harry Potter

1. d	27. g	53. d	79. b
2. h	28. b	54. a	80. a
3. f	29. c	55. b	81. c
4. a	30. c	56. f	82. d
5. g	31. d	57. d	83. e
6. e	32. e	58. e	84. b
7. b	33. f	59. g	85. a
8. c	34. b	60. a	86. c
9. c	35. a	61. b	87. d
10. e	36. i	62. c	88. e
11. a	37. f	63. c	89. b
12. g	38. g	64. b	90. a
13. f	39. h	65. e	91. d
14. d	40. b	66. a	92. e
15. b	41. c	67. d	93. f
16. f	42. e	68. d	94. g
17. e	43. a	69. c	95. h
18. g	44. d	70. a	96. c
19. c	45. d	71. b	97. b
20. a	46. f	72. c	98. a
21. b	47. g	73. d	99. b
22. d	48. e	74. e	100. c
23. d	49. b	75. b	101. e
24. e	50. c	76. a	102. f
25. a	51. a	77. c	103. d
26. f	52. c	78. d	104. a

DAILY LESSONS

Lesson One

Objectives
1. To introduce the unit on **Harry Potter and the Sorcerer's Stone**
2. To distribute books and other related materials (study guides, reading assignments, etc.)
3. To prepare students to discover the concept of belonging via a bulletin board activity
4. To prepare a bulletin board activity demonstrating belonging

Activity #1
Explain briefly to the students why you have chosen **Harry Potter and the Sorcerer's Stone** as a book for them to read. Try to make them understand why you think they will enjoy and learn from the book and the characters and experiences in it.

Despite the popularity of the whole Harry Potter phenomenon, there are, of course, many detractors of this series of books. Although both children and adults have been drawn to the Potter series, there are in our communities parents, religious leaders, educators, and other community members who believe that the Harry Potter series–with its emphasis on wizardry and the occult–is unfit to be taught in our public schools. Certainly these folks are entitled to their opinions, even though many other people disagree with them.

If you think you might be challenged on your choice of a Harry Potter book as a unit of study in your classroom, it might be helpful to you to focus your thinking on the subject early on. In this writer's opinion, it is very possible to view the wizardry and occult interest in the book as a metaphor. Harry, a bright, talented child who is underappreciated by many of the adults and nearly all of the children in his world, has spent ten unhappy years in the company of his aunt and uncle, Vernon and Petunia Dursley, and his spoiled cousin, Dudley.

What Harry discovers once Hagrid shows up to claim him as a Hogwarts student is a community in which he is prized, a venue in which he can test and hone his skills and values and can shine as an individual, a student, an athlete, and a loyal friend. At Hogwarts, Harry, although being famous even before his arrival, is asked to prove himself. And that he does. Through the beginning of his first year at the famous wizardry school, Harry makes a variety of moral choices and emerges by the Christmas holidays much more sure of himself and secure in the world around him. He is on his way to assuming his rightful role as a member of the larger community.

For those who feel that the wizardry and witchcraft in the book challenge their religious beliefs, I offer no challenges to their way of thinking. Personal religious beliefs are just that, and I would be among the last people to *inflict* the Harry Potter books on them. Were I able, I would ask only that they would read at least one of the books and try to see it for the fantasy that it is. If there are *light* arts as well as *dark* ones, Harry and his chosen companions and adult friends are clearly on the side of light. It is hard not to celebrate his many victories–as a boy and as a wizard.

Lesson One - **Harry Potter** - page 2

Having said all of that, do spend time with your students discussing your choice of this book. In fact, you probably will want to indulge some discussion of the entire Harry Potter phenomenon and the way that it fits into our current national needs, desires, and mood.

Activity #2
Distribute the materials students will use in this unit. Explain in detail how students are to use the materials.

Study Guides Students should read the study guide questions for each reading assignment before beginning the assignment to get a feel for what events and ideas are important in the section they are about to read. After reading the section, students will (as a class, in small groups, or individually) answer the questions to review the important events and ideas from that section of the book. Students should keep the study guides as study materials for the unit test.

Vocabulary As they are reading a section of the text, students will do vocabulary work related to the section they are reading. If they hunt for the vocabulary words as they read, students should be able to figure out the contextual meaning of the words. Following the completion of the reading of the book, there will be a vocabulary review of all the words used in the vocabulary assignments. Students should keep their vocabulary work as study materials for the unit test.

Reading Assignment Sheet You need to fill in the reading assignment sheet to let students know when their reading has to be completed. You can either write the assignment on a side chalk board or bulletin board and leave it there for students to see each day, or you can make copies for each student to have. In any case, advise students to become very familiar with the reading assignments so they know what is expected of them.

Extra Activities Center The Unit Resource portion of this unit contains suggestions for a library of related books and articles in your classroom as well as crossword and word search puzzles. Make a center in your room where you will keep these materials for students to use. (Bring the books and articles in from the library and keep several copies of the puzzles on hand.) Explain to students that these materials are available for their use when they finish reading assignments or other class work early.

Nonfiction Assignment Sheet Nonfiction Assignment Sheet Explain to students that they each are to read at least one nonfiction piece from the in-class library or elsewhere at some time during the unit. They might want to take a book out of the school library (if such books are available for circulation), use a book in the school library, use a book in a local community library, or refer to books that they already have in their homes. Students will fill out a nonfiction assignment sheet after completing the reading to help you evaluate their reading experiences and to help the students to think about and evaluate their own reading.

Lesson One - **Harry Potter** - page 3

Books Each school has its own rules and regulations regarding student use of school books. Advise students of the procedures that are usual for your school.

Activity #3
Ask students to think of a time when they felt that they did or did not belong. For the next class meeting, they may present a hand-drawn picture of how they felt when a part of a group or when they did not. They may bring a cut-out picture from a magazine or newspaper which depicts how they felt or present a poem or a couple of paragraphs explaining their aloneness.

The point is not to create great works of art but instead to get students to thinking of belonging and not belonging as Harry Potter, the hero of **Harry Potter and the Sorcerer's Stone** experiences it. If you get some interesting expressions, you might like to post them on the bulletin board–with or without names. If you don't get pictures or writing appropriate to put on the bulletin board, you might bring in a few pictures yourself. In fact, it usually helps to begin the construction of the bulletin board activity yourself and then encourage students to join in.

Activity #4
You will want to set the bulletin board up in such a way that students will have occasion to look at it each day that they are reading the novel.

Nonfiction Assignment Sheet - Harry Potter
(To be completed after reading the required nonfiction article)

Name _____ Date _____ Class _____

Title of Nonfiction Read _____

Author _____ Publication Date _____

I. **Factual Summary**: Write a short summary of the piece you read.

II. **Vocabulary**:
    1. Which vocabulary words were difficult?

    2. What did you do to help yourself understand the words?

III. **Interpretation**: What was the main point the author wanted you to get from reading his or her work?

IV. **Criticism**:
    1. Which points of the piece did you agree with or find easy to believe? Why?

    2. Which points did you disagree with or find hard to believe? Why?

V. **Personal Response**:
    1. What do you think about this piece of writing overall?

    2. How does this piece help you better understand the book, **Harry Potter and the Sorcerer's Stone**?

Oral Reading Evaluation - Harry Potter

Name _____ Class _____ Date _____

SKILL	EXCELLENT	GOOD	AVERAGE	FAIR	POOR
Fluency	5	4	3	2	1
Clarity	5	4	3	2	1
Audibility	5	4	3	2	1
Pronunciation	5	4	3	2	1
_____	5	4	3	2	1
_____	5	4	3	2	1

Total _____   Grade _____

Comments:

Lesson Two

Objectives
1. To preview the study questions for Chapter One
2. To familiarize students with the vocabulary for Chapter One

Activity #1
Preview the study questions and have students look over the vocabulary words for Chapter One of **Harry Potter.** If students do not finish this assignment during the class period, they should complete it, including the vocabulary worksheets, prior to the next class meeting.

Activity #2
Spend a brief time making sure that students have become familiar with the vocabulary words for Chapter One.

Lesson Three

Objectives
1. To begin consideration and discussion of one theme in **Harry Potter**, namely belonging vs not belonging
2. To read pp 1-17 aloud as a class
3. To give students practice reading orally
4. To evaluate students' oral reading
5. To preview the study questions for Chapter Two, pp 18-30

Activity #1
You might begin by discussing the idea of what it means to belong–to a family, to a group, to a community, to a country. Try to get the students to think about and discuss their feelings about being part of an entity larger than themselves. How does it feel to belong? What rights does one acquire when one belongs? What responsibilities?

For the first three chapters of **Harry Potter**, Harry does **not** belong. Not only is he not a part of his milieu, but he is resented and decidedly unwanted. His parents were different, and so is he. But he has no means of comparing how he feels to how he might feel until he is rescued from the Dursleys and admitted to Hogwarts.

Lesson Three - **Harry Potter** - page 2

How does it feel to *not* belong? Perhaps you might encourage expression of who and who does not belong in your school. What does it feel like to belong or to *not* belong at school? Is it important that a person feels a sense of belonging *everywhere*, or is it only important that a person belong *somewhere*? Is it even important to belong anywhere? Is it possible to be different and still belong? There are no right or wrong points of view here. If students grasp in a number of ways the idea of belonging–and also the idea of alienation--they will be better able to consider Harry Potter's life and overall existence.

Activity #2
Have students read pp 1-17 out loud in class. You probably know the best way to choose readers from your class: pick students at random, ask for volunteers, or use whatever other method works best for your group. If you have not yet completed an oral reading evaluation for your students this marking period, this would be a good opportunity to do so. A form is included with this unit for your convenience. It probably is a good idea to share with students ahead of time the ways in which you are evaluating their reading skills. Try to make time to share your evaluations with students.

There should be enough time to complete all of the reading. However, if students do not complete reading through pp 1-17 in class, they should do so prior to your next class meeting.

Activity #3
Begin previewing the student questions and doing the pre-reading vocabulary work for Chapter Two. If you run out of time for the study questions and vocabulary work, tell students that they should have completed these tasks prior to the next class meeting.

Activity #4
Spend just a minute or two calling students' attention to the bulletin board materials that stress Harry Potter's growing sense of belonging.

Lesson Four

Objectives
1.   To recap the study questions and vocabulary from the last class
2.   To review the main events and ideas from Chapter One
3.   To read Chapter Two in class
4.   To do an in-class activity exploring family and community dynamics

Activity #1
Spend just enough time on the study questions and vocabulary to ensure that students are understanding the assignment and to prepare them for the reading in class.

Activity #2
Briefly review the main events and ideas from Chapter One. Continue to examine the ideas of belonging and being different. In addition to any vocabulary words, you might ask students to pick out words in the text that stress these ideas.

Activity #3
Have students read Chapter Two of **Harry Potter** out loud in class. Use the method of selecting student readers that works best for you. Continue the oral reading evaluations. Continue to share your evaluations with students, especially if students need a lot of improvement or if they demonstrate dramatic improvement.

Activity #4
Spend a little time with students exploring family and community dynamics. What is the ideal family, the ideal community, and how does the individual fit into them? In students' opinions, what types of family and/or community units are best. Have them choose three or four words or phrases which describe a good family or a good community. Then spend a short time in class allowing students to explain and defend their choice of words and/or phrases.

Lesson Five

Objectives
1.	To review the main events and ideas from Chapter Two
2,	To do study questions for Chapter Three
3.	To do vocabulary work for Chapter Three
4.	To assign the reading for Chapter Three

Activity #1
Briefly review the main events and ideas from Chapter Two. Try to be sure that students are following the plot development.

Activity #2
Do the preview work for Chapter Four: study questions and vocabulary

Activity #3
Assign Chapter Three to be read at home.

Lesson Six

Objective
	To give students the opportunity to write to inform/explain

Activity #1
Have students complete Writing Assignment #1 (Writing to Inform/Explain). The directions for the assignment follow. Because we have so far read only the first few chapters of **Harry Potter**, we will focus on not belonging, on not being a part of things, on being excluded. The first writing assignment will focus on that point of view.

Try to get the students' compositions back to them as soon as you can so that they can receive pointers on their writing. They will be writing another composition–this time at home–for Lesson Ten.

Writing Assignment #1 - Harry Potter
(Writing to Inform/Explain)

PROMPT
In the first three chapters of **Harry Potter**, J. K. Rowling has made it clear that Harry Potter is living in a community where he is not accepted. So far, we might examine this community in terms of the physical environment of the house on Privet Lane, the cupboard at the bottom of the stairs, the second bedroom, the family members and other people with whom Harry interacts, and his general life situation/culture (everything that made up his life prior to his first meeting with the giant Hagrid).

Your assignment is to write a composition to explain to the reader that Harry Potter has consistently been alienated from his own family, school, and community. Harry, at the beginning of the book, has no sense of belonging. Although you should talk about each of the aspects of the Harry's life (physical environment, people in the Dursleys' neighborhood, people associated with Hogwarts, and Harry's life situation), you may introduce them in any order. Just be sure to give examples supporting each aspect and showing that Harry is living in a hostile environment.

It might help to pretend that your reader has not read the first three chapters of the book. Your job is to demonstrate to the reader that Harry's world, at least in this first part of the book, is diametrically opposed to a sense of belonging.

PREWRITING
Begin by quickly re-reading the first three chapters of the book. Make some notes as you re-read. Think about what it would be like to **be** Harry, about how he feels about his dead parents, his home life, the events that have taken him to the place where he lives, and about the people he encounters there and at Hogwarts.

DRAFTING
Write an introductory paragraph designed to catch the reader's attention and to state your composition's main point: that Harry Potter is living in a world that alienates him. Write at least one paragraph discussing each aspect of that world that you choose to consider. Make sure that you give sufficient examples and that you are not simply quoting from the book. Write a concluding summary paragraph.

PROMPT
When you finish the rough draft of your paper, ask a student who sits near you to read it and to see if your main point is clearly expressed and supported by good examples. Then the student should tell you what he or she liked best about your work, which parts were difficult to understand, and ways in which your work could be improved. Re-read your paper considering your critic's comments and make the corrections you think are necessary.

Writing Evaluation Form - Harry Potter

Name _____   Date _____

Writing Assignment _____   Grade _____

Circle One for each item:

Topic interest	excellent	good	fair	poor
Overall organization	excellent	good	fair	poor
Clarity of expression	excellent	good	fair	poor
Grammar	excellent	good	fair	poor
Spelling	excellent	good	fair	poor
Punctuation	excellent	good	fair	poor

Strengths

Weaknesses

Comments/Suggestions

Lesson Seven

Objectives
1. To review Chapter Three
2. To have students write one paragraph about a single main point in Chapter Three
3. To do the preview work for Chapter Four: study questions and vocabulary

Activity #1
Review with students the main events of Chapter Three.

Activity #2
Have the students write one paragraph about a main point in Chapter Three, which they now have read and reviewed. The objects of writing the paragraph are to keep the students writing and to further clarify their understanding of the pages they have read. Some points that they might consider–if they don't easily come up with points themselves–are the differences in the educational situations of Harry and his cousin Dudley, the Dursleys' overreaction to the letters that arrive at the house for Harry, Mr. Dursley's inability to lead his family away from danger, the special abilities of the people sending the letters, Mr. Dursley's willingness to put his family in real danger in order to escape from perceived danger, and the way that the author (Rowling) builds up suspense throughout the chapter to the BOOM that marks Hagrid's arrival

Activity #3
This time you might have the students work in small groups to do the preview work for Chapter Four. If time permits, you might want to circulate among the groups to be sure that most of the students are participating.

Lesson Eight

<u>Objectives</u>
1. To read Chapter Four in class
2. To discuss in class one aspect of Chapter Four
3. To do the preview work for Chapter Five: study questions and vocabulary
4. To assign Chapter Five to be read at home

<u>Activity #1</u>
In order to vary the class readings, you might try going student by student, having each one read one sentence from **Harry Potter**. Thus, a student would read, "The escape of the Brazilian boa constrictor earned Harry his longest-ever punishment." Then the second student would read, "By the time he was allowed out of his cupboard again, the summer holidays had started and Dudley had already broken his new video camera, crashed his remote control airplane, and, first time out on his racing bike, knocked down old Mrs. Figg as she crossed Privet Drive on her crutches." The next student would read, "Harry was glad school was over, but there was no escaping Dudley's gang, who visited the house every single day." And so on until the class collectively has read Chapter Four.

If you choose this method of reading out loud, you might also encourage the students to read with real feeling–an easy task given the fun of having a giant cow the Dursleys and thrill Harry.

If you prefer simply to have students read out loud as you have done in earlier activities, that's fine too. Do what seems best for your students. Sometimes some variety will help to keep students' attention focused better.

<u>Activity #2</u>
Although you and the students may wish to discuss other issues in this chapter, one of the most interesting might be the effect that Hagrid's presence has on each of the characters–Harry, Mr. and Mrs. Dursley, and Dudley. Students should readily be able to see how Hagrid brings out the worst in the Dursleys and the best in Harry. It's not hard to see how Mr. Dursley blusters and tries to assert himself. Mrs. Dursley, on the other hand, seizes the opportunity to shriek about her "dratted sister." Ultimately, though, both of them are silenced–Harry "had almost forgotten that the Dursleys were there." Mr. Dursley makes one last-ditch effort to assert himself, but Hagrid cows him by adding a pig's tail to Dudley, and all three Dursleys wind up fleeing the room.

Harry is a different story. Faced with all kinds of startling information about himself and his parents, he keeps his wits about him throughout. He isn't afraid so much as curious. And, as the pieces start to fall into place for him, he seems to accept information that a short time ago would have been totally unthinkable. Try to get your students to discuss *their* response to this chapter. It may or may not be exactly what has been described in the two paragraphs above. But, it is pretty much guaranteed that they will have cheered Hagrid on all the way as the Dursleys finally got their due. This should be a fun discussion.

Lesson Eight - **Harry Potter** - page 2

<u>Activity #3</u>
If time permits, do the preview work for Chapter Five in class. If time is short, ask students to complete the preview work at home and to bring it to the next class.

<u>Activity #4</u>
Assign Chapter Five to be read at home. Chapter Five is the longest the students have had to read so far, so you might want to encourage them to read it early and carefully. From time to time, you might also encourage students to read out loud at home, either for themselves or to a friend, a sibling, a parent, or whatever.

Lesson Nine

Objectives
1. To make sure that students are keeping up
2. To review Chapter Five
3. To discuss favorite characters with students
4. To prepare students for the Nonfiction Reading Assignment

Activity #1
See if students have any questions about the preview work that they have been doing in and out of class. Take a few minutes for responses if necessary. Try to be sure that all students are understanding the book. This is a good time to note any students who aren't doing their work on a regular basis and to try to get them on track.

You may be collecting these preview exercises: if so, be sure that they are returned to students promptly for study purposes.

Activity #2
Review Chapter Five that students have read at home.

Activity #3
Perhaps the easiest and most beneficial way to get this discussion going is to ask students to choose their favorite character. When they have chosen–individually or as a group–try to get them to articulate *why* they chose as they did. Is their character strong? Funny? Like someone they already know? Someone they might choose as a friend? Someone that it is fun to see put in his or her place? If they had to choose one character as a friend, who would it be? Are the Dursleys in fact "perfectly normal"? What is "normal" becoming in **Harry Potter**?

The most important purpose of the discussion is, of course, to encourage students to read closely and to think about the characters and their roles in the book. They should be able to do more than tell you that Hagrid is "cool" or "scary" or that Harry is "awesome." Push them for details. Make them refer back to the text to support their views.

Activity #4
Spend some time discussing the purposes and topics of the nonfiction reading assignment. Some purposes for doing the nonfiction reading are to enhance the students' knowledge, to supplement what they are learning through reading **Harry Potter**, to encourage them to read on their own, and to make the book even more relevant to real life.

Topics to Choose for Nonfiction Reading Assignment - Harry Potter

You may want to choose from the following list of topics for your Nonfiction Reading Assignment. All of the topics are based in some way on **Harry Potter and the Sorcerer's Stone**. This is far from a complete list. There must be hundreds of topics that might prove interesting. You may want to pick a different topic altogether.

However, regardless of the topic you choose, you must clear your choice with your teacher *before you begin the assignment*. Between you and your teacher, you will be able to choose a topic that is relevant, manageable, and appropriate for you.

1. The movie (Harry Potter and the Sorcerer's Stone)
   (read *about* the movie: how hard or difficult it was to make, how popular it is/was, how the actors and actresses were chosen to play the roles, the involvement of J.K. Rowling in making the film, how true to the book the film is or isn't, etc.)

2. The history of wizardry and witchcraft
   (what wizards are, if they really exist, people's views of wizardry and witchcraft now, their views in the past, American witchcraft trials, etc.)

3. Modern magicians
   (Houdini, David Copperfield, etc., special magic "tricks," sleight of hand, etc.)

4. Unicorns, Goblins, Trolls, Centaurs, and Dragons
   (research one of these creatures of folklore and legendary mythology)

5. Ghosts
   (do they exist? who thinks so? are there places thought to be haunted? do ghosts haunt graveyards?)

6. Halloween
   (where did the holiday come from? why do we celebrate it today? what does it mean today? do some religions disapprove of Halloween? why? is the holiday becoming problematic for children and parents today? why are black cats associated with Halloween?)

7. Stones
   (the power of stones, the worship of sacred stones, gravestones as markers, Stonehenge in England, the Blarney Stone, etc.)

8. Cloaks
   (worn by wizards, magicians, and kings; Superman's cape; Joseph's Coat of Many Colors)

Nonfiction Reading Assignment - **Harry Potter** - page 2

9. Fairy Tales
   (Cinderella, Hansel and Gretel, Snow White, and others)

10. The Private School
    (in the past, today, in literature, etc.)

11. The hero in myth and literature
    (Oedipus, Odysseus, Zeus, King Arthur, Sir Gawain, Beowulf, Hercules, Orpheus, etc.)

12. Book Awards
    (research *Publisher's Weekly* Best Book, *USA Today* Bestseller, and ALA Notable Book awards; Gold Medal Smarties Prize; and possibly others)

Lesson Ten

Objectives
1. To give students additional time to discuss and begin research on the Nonfiction Reading Assignment
2. To give students the opportunity to write–at home this time–to express a personal opinion
3. To do the preview work in class for Chapter Six: short answer and vocabulary
4. To assign Chapter Six to be read at home

Activity #1
If time allows, have students announce to the class what they intend to do for their Nonfiction Reading Assignment. Also, this might be a god time to review the appropriateness or inappropriateness of students' topic choices. You might need individual meetings with students if they lean toward topics that you believe are inappropriate for them in some way. Give students time to do some further reading for the assignment.

Activity #2
Make Writing Assignment #2. For this assignment, students will write a brief news story (or stories) on their choice of topics. The writing will test their ability to express themselves clearly and to pay attention to specific details.

If for any reason you believe the assignment is too short or too simplistic for your class, you may either modify it or ask the students to write on several topics. Writing Assignment #2 was created so that it would be able to be adapted to student audiences at a variety of reading and writing levels.

The directions for Writing Assignment #2 follow.

Activity #3
Do the preview work in class for Chapter Six.

Activity #4
Assign Chapter Six to be read at home.

Writing Assignment #2 - Harry Potter
(Writing a News Story)

PROMPT

Based on the reading you have done so far in **Harry Potter and the Sorcerer's Stone,** you are to write a news story about some situation (or situations) in the book's first six chapters. The object is to make believe that some incident or incidents have been discovered and that a reporter is covering them in the local press. Your job is to express yourself very clearly and to use a lot of specific details in order to convey the points you want to make. You will write on one or more of the following topics, as assigned by your teacher. Each topic should require at least two or three paragraphs.

1) It has been discovered–prior to Hagrid's appearance--that Harry Potter is living with the Dursleys. Pretend that you are a news reporter who has learned about the situation. You have been allowed to interview all parties. Now you want to write about their story in the local paper. Use as much information as possible from the text. You may speculate, but you must make clear what is fact (from the book) and what is speculation (your opinions).

2) It has been discovered that a giant named Hagrid has broken into a hut occupied by Petunia and Vernon Dursley, their son Dudley, and their nephew Harry Potter. Hagrid claims that he is from a school called Hogwarts School of Witchcraft and Wizardry, and he intends to take Harry Potter with him to be outfitted for attendance at the school–against the wishes of Harry's guardians, the Dursleys. Write a news item about the case for the local paper.

3) Pretend that Professor Dumbledore, Hagrid, and Professor McGonagall are discovered in Privet Drive with the young Harry Potter. The police arrive. The trio says that they are delivering Harry Potter to his aunt and uncle because his parents have been killed in a blast. All three claim to be employed by a school called Hogwarts School of Witchcraft and Wizardry. Write a news item about the situation for the local paper.

4) Pretend that someone has spotted the Weasleys and Harry Potter at the railway station near platforms nine and ten. Somehow they look suspicious. You have noticed that Harry Potter has been standing around the station for quite some time eyeing the two platforms and watching people come and go. Suddenly he begins talking with the Weasleys. The police are called, and it becomes obvious that all of the children are carrying an assortment of odd things, such as wands, owls, broomsticks, and other paraphernalia. Write a news item about the police discovery for the local paper.

5) Pretend that Hagrid and Harry have lost the list of items needed to outfit Harry for Hogwarts. The list is found by a local citizen who sends it along to the local newspaper. With no more information than the list itself, write a news item for the newspaper about the unusual discovery.

Writing Assignment #2 - **Harry Potter** - page 2

> You may speculate about the list in any way that you believe a reporter would do. Be sure to tell how the list was found, what the finder thought about it, and what the reporter thinks of it.

6) Write a news story about the escape of the boa constrictor from the tank at the zoo. Use the basic information from the text. Tell the story in whatever way you believe would be interesting to the readers of the local paper. For this story, you may assume that you have been privy to everything that happened at the zoo.

PREWRITING

Decide how you want to approach this assignment. Choose one or more options (as assigned by your teacher). For each news story that you write, figure out how you want to approach the story. It may be serious, funny, or a combination of both. Whichever options are chosen, you should fill your news story with lots of specific details.

DRAFTING

Write a draft of the story. Try to make it interesting enough that you would bother to read it if it appeared in your local newspaper. Give specific examples. You might like to look at some news briefs in your paper as you begin drafting this assignment.

PROMPT

When you finish the draft of your paper, ask someone to read it and see if you have written it as well as possible. Your reader may be a friend, classmate, family member, or anyone else who might be a good reviewer. After reading your rough draft, he or she should tell you what he or she liked best about your work, which parts were difficult to understand, and ways in which your work could be improved. Reread your paper considering your critic's comments and make the corrections you think are necessary.

PROOFREADING

Do a final proofreading of your paper, double-checking your grammar, spelling, and organization of ideas.

Lesson Eleven

Objectives
1. To discuss briefly Chapter Six
2. To set parameters for the Project
3. To do the preview work for Chapter Seven

Activity #1
Discuss briefly Chapter Six. Make sure that students have an opportunity to ask any questions that may have occurred to them. The plot gets a little more complicated as the book progresses. Try to see that no one is lost at this early point.

Activity #2
Introduce Project Modern Magic to your students (details on the next page). Remember that this is an optional project. If you choose not to include it in your planning, you might instead assign the students to choose their favorite **Harry Potter** character and write a composition that describes that character and explains why they chose him or her. Instead of calling the writing a composition or essay, you might allow students to put their ideas in the form of a letter to a friend. They might, that is, be writing to tell a friend about an interesting person they have met. You might also ask the students to present their writing to the whole class.

Activity #3
Do the preview work for Chapter Seven: short answer and vocabulary

Project Modern Magic

Objectives
Project Modern Magic is a total class project for use in conjunction with the book **Harry Potter and the Sorcerer's Stone** by J. K. Rowling. Since one of the main ideas in the book is the use of witchcraft and wizardry, this is a good opportunity to acquaint students with modern magic and the role it plays in our society. Everyone today has seen someone doing magic tricks, either in person or on television or in the movies. David Copperfield, an illusionist, is a good professional example. But probably everyone has seen someone do "magic tricks." Maybe they involved cards or maybe they seemed to make something or someone disappear.

But at some level, these "tricks" satisfy our need for wonderment. We all seem to have a need to experience something that science says shouldn't be possible. And even though we acknowledge that we are watching a "trick," in many cases the "trick" is the art of sleight of hand, misdirection, etc. One of the most common features of modern magic tricks is the utilization of patter, that is, the magician talks a blue streak of constant description of what he or she is going to do. While we are intent on paying attention to the pattern, he or she is in fact setting up the trick without our knowledge. In many cases, when a contemporary magician pulls up one sleeve to show you that there is nothing hidden there, you would be wise to watch his other hand or extremities for tell-tale movement. The fun is in trying to spot the "trick."

For this project, students may use books to find useful information, or they may use the Internet if they have easy access to computers. If possible, students may even choose to interview a local magician if such a person exists in your town.

THE PROJECT
This project is separate from the rest of the unit on **Harry Potter**, so you can either use it while you are reading and reviewing the book or as a separate mini-unit after you have completed the unit tests for **Harry Potter**. Also, having it as a separate project enables you to either eliminate it or to use it, without disturbing the flow of the unit as a whole.

Assignment #1
Your local television station or newspaper should have some articles in their archives on modern magicians. And, of course, you yourself might use the Internet if computer availability is not a problem. At any rate, try to find a few articles/reports on magic/magicians and show them to your students. Use the reports and articles as a springboard to a discussion of the students' view of magic.

Assignment #2
As a class, write a letter to a local magician inviting him or her to come to your class to discuss magic and perhaps to perform a few tricks. You probably can find such a person in your local telephone book, perhaps under Children's Parties or such. Even if such a person doesn't exist in your community,

Project Modern Magic - **Harry Potter** - page 2

there surely is someone nearby who knows how to do some parlor tricks and would be willing to share his or her expertise with your students. Send the letter and then make any necessary follow-up phone calls to make arrangements for the visit.

Activity #3
After students have the information you gather on magic, send them to the library to do some research. One interesting person to investigate, for instance, might be Harry Houdini, the famous escape artist. Information should be available on Houdini in either your school library or your local library. It certainly is available on the Internet.

Divide your students into groups and have each group investigate some aspect of Houdini's life and craft. They might, for example, find out about his personal life. They might want to research the kind of escapes he did and the close calls he had. They might also investigate Houdini's beliefs in a life after death: he, after all, had promised that he would communicate back to this world from the next if he possibly could. One of your groups could research even one of the escapes he did and explain it to the rest of the class with possible suggestions about how Houdini might have accomplished it.

Assignment #4
After student have done their research, have them give brief oral reports about their reading whenever appropriate. That way, all students can be exposed to the wealth of information that has been collected.

Assignment #5
Host the person who was invited to class in Assignment #2. Should you not have been able to find even one person to do some tricks for your class, you might investigate getting a card game from a local store and inviting students to learn some tricks. Check your local phone book for magic stores and supplies.

One of the purposes of this project obviously is to have fun. Your students will be doing sufficient writing and research during other parts of the unit on **Harry Potter**. For this project, they might be allowed simply to enjoy learning about some aspects of modern magic and perhaps even trying their hand as being "magicians" as well.

Lesson Twelve

Objectives
1. To read Chapter Seven in class and to evaluate student reading
2. To review the main ideas, events, and characterizations in the first seven chapters of **Harry Potter**
3. To have students exercise their critical thinking skills

Activity #1
Choose students to read out loud Chapter Seven. Use the evaluation form if you choose to do so.

Activity #2
Review with students the main ideas, events, and characterizations in the first seven chapters of **Harry Potter**.

(The first two objectives in Lesson Twelve should be achieved easily and rather quickly. This is a good time to be sure that all students are keeping up with the story line, main ideas, and characterizations in the book.)

Activity #3
Choose some questions from the Extra Discussion Questions/Writing Assignments which seem most appropriate for your students. A class discussion of these questions is most effective if students have been given the opportunity to formulate answers to the questions prior to the discussion. To this end, you may either have all the students formulate answers to all the questions you choose, divide your class into groups and assign one or more questions to each group, or assign one question to each student in your class. The option you choose will make a difference in the amount of class time needed for this activity.

After students have had ample time to formulate answers to the questions, begin your class discussion of the questions and the ideas presented by them. Be sure students take notes during the discussion so they have information to study for the unit test.

A word of warning: You will not want your students to see some of these discussion questions and quotations until they have completed the whole book. Seeing them would give the plot away to students when they are only partway through **Harry Potter**.

Extra Discussion Questions/Writing Assignments - Harry Potter

Interpretive

1. With whom are you supposed to be sympathizing while reading **Harry Potter**? Does the author "stack the deck" when she gives you details about what happens? Did you sympathize with and like some characters more than others? Why do you think that was true?

2. How different are the characters in **Harry Potter** from each other? Is each character distinctly drawn? Do you feel that you would recognize each character were you to meet him or her? How so?

3. What are the main conflicts in the book, and how are they being resolved?

4. How are some of the events of **Harry Potter** foreshadowed? Do you know right from the beginning of the book that Harry's fortunes are subject to change? Do you expect something extraordinary to happen to him?

5. Give as complete a character analysis of Harry as possible. Explain what kind of person he is, how smart you think he might be, etc.

6. How does Rowling go about building the suspense in the book? Is it, in fact, suspenseful? As you finish each chapter, are you anxious to know what happens next?

Critical

7. Explain the significance of each of the book's chapter titles (at least as far as you have read so far). Are the titles descriptive enough? Do they indicate what will happen in each chapter?

8. Is there another title that could be used for the whole book? **Harry Potter and the Sorcerer's Stone** is literally descriptive, but could it have been more exciting or more mysterious? Should it have been either?

9. Compare and contrast Harry Potter and Dudley Dursley.

10. What is life like for Dudley? What do you think he will be like when he's forty years old?

11. In real life, do you think Uncle Vernon Dursley would have phoned the police when Hagrid showed up? How realistic is what actually happened in the book? Should the book be more realistic? If not, why not?

Extra Discussion - **Harry Potter** - page 2

Personal Response

12. If you had to pick one character to spend time with, who would it be?

13. If you knew Harry personally before Hagrid showed up, would you be inclined to try to help him? What if you knew how he was being treated and how he was sleeping in a cupboard under the stairs? What would your responsibility be to him?

14. What is the value of having someone who is true to his word? How important is it to be able to rely on other people? How important is it to feel liked, or even loved?

15. How would you feel if you were Harry when Hagrid showed up?

Quotations

16. "Er — Petunia, dear — you haven't heard from your sister lately, have you?"

17. "Really, Dumbledore, you think you can explain all this in a letter? These people will never understand him! He'll be famous — a legend — I wouldn't be surprised if today was known as Harry Potter day in the future — there will be books written about Harry — every child in our world will known his name!"

18. "I would trust Hagrid with my life," said Dumbledore.

19. "No, sir — house was almost destroyed, but I got him out all right before the Muggles started swarmin' around. He fell asleep as we was flyin' over Bristol."

20. "To Harry Potter — the boy who lived!"

21. "They stuff people's heads down the toilet the first day at Stonewall," he told Harry.

22. "Ah, shut up, Dursley, yeh great prune...."

23. "....It so happens that the phoenix whose tail feather is in your wand, gave another feather — just one other. It is very curious indeed that you should be destined for this wand when its brother — why, its brother gave you that scar."

24. "Well, there you are, boy. Platform nine — platform ten. Your platform should be somewhere in the middle, but they don't seem to have built it yet, do they?"

Extra Discussion - **Harry Potter** - page 3

25. "All you have to do is walk straight at the barrier between platforms nine and ten. Don't stop and don't be scared you'll crash into it, that's very important...."

26. "His name's Scabbers and he's useless, he hardly ever wakes up. Percy got an owl from my dad for being made a prefect, but they couldn't aff — I mean, I got Scabbers instead."

27. "Potter, this is Oliver Wood. Wood — I've found you a Seeker."

28. "You're saying it wrong....It's Wing-*gar*-dium Levi-*o*-sa, make the 'gar' nice and long."

29. "....It does not do to dwell on dreams and forget to live, remember that...."

30. "Well — yeah — how many three-headed dogs d'yeh meet, even around Hogwarts? So I told him, Fluffy's a piece o' cake if yeh know how to calm him down, jus' play him a bit o' music an' he'll go straight off ter sleep — "

31. "HAVE YOU GONE MAD?" Ron bellowed. "ARE YOU A WITCH OR NOT?"

32. "Yes ..." said Ron softly, "it's the only way ... I've got to be taken."

33. "See what I have become?" the face said. "Mere shadow and vapor ... I have form only when I can share another's body ... but there have always been those willing to let me into their hearts and minds ...."

34. "Your mother died to save you. If there's one thing Voldemort cannot understand, it is love...."

35. "....You see, only one who wanted to *find* the Stone — find it, but not use it — would be able to get it, otherwise they'd just see themselves making gold or drinking Elixir of Life...."

36. "There are all kinds of courage," said Dumbledore, smiling. "It takes a great deal of bravery to stand up to our enemies, but just as much to stand up to our friends...."

Lesson Thirteen

Objectives
1. To assign the preview work for Chapter Eight to be done at home
2. To assign Chapter Eight to be read at home
3. To do a role-playing exercise

Activity #1
Assign the preview work for Chapter Eight: short answer and vocabulary.

Activity #2
Assign Chapter Eight to be read at home.

Activity #3
The role-playing exercise is designed to help the students to understand the characters in **Harry Potter** better by envisioning them in different contexts. Except for making the assignments in Activities #1 and #2, try to put aside one entire class to achieve Objective 3. What you are going to do is ask some of your students to do some role playing in front of the rest of the class. Because not everyone will have the opportunity to play a role in class, the other students will learn from observing. Both actors and observers should be encouraged to think about how the characters are going to act in each scenario. You will be the best judge of which students can be relied on to carry out the assignment with a reasonable degree of understanding and comfort.

Don't worry that you don't have enough time to accommodate this kind of role playing. Its object is not to rehearse or spend a lot of time preparing for the role playing. It is, instead, to think through very quickly how a character will act based on which students already know about him or her.

This activity will work best if you try to prepare the students to have a good time doing it. Make sure they realize that there is no totally right or totally wrong way to do the activity. Instead, they should listen closely to the scenarios that you lay out, think very quickly about how each assigned character would react to each, and then pretend to *be* that character to the best of their ability.

Choose the scenarios that you think your students will best understand. You may do only one of the scenarios or all three. If you want, you can even makeup new scenarios, with or without your students' help. Again, there is no right or wrong here. You are just moving the characters around a little bit in order to let students look at them a little differently and understand them a little bit better.

Read the scenario. Give students three to five minutes to prepare, and then give them five minutes or less to act out the scenario. The ONLY requirement is that students try as hard as possible to keep the character as he or she behaved in the pages assigned so far in **Harry Potter**.

Lesson Thirteen - **Harry Potter** - page 2

Scenario #1 Hagrid and Dumbledore
Assume that Dumbledore has seen everything that happened in the hut between Hagrid and the Dursleys–as well he might have. He loves Hagrid, but he becomes exasperated with him from time to time because Hagrid continues to do things that he knows he isn't supposed to do. **Have Dumbledore "scold" Hagrid appropriately and give Hagrid ample time to respond.**

Scenario #2 Mr. and Mrs. Dursley
Despite all his bluffing, let's suppose that Mr. Dursley sees that they might finally be rid of Harry altogether. He hasn't, after all, wanted Harry to live with them, and he has always seen Harry as a burden. ***Have Mr. Dursley express his feelings directly to Mrs. Dursley and have her respond–but remember that her major concern will be what might happen if people find out what she has done.***

Scenario #3 James and Lily Potter and Harry
Of course, James and Lily Potter never had the opportunity to say goodbye to Harry. Pretend that they are able somehow to talk directly to him and to explain what happened to them and why. ***Give the Potters time to speak and then have Harry respond to them.***

Scenario #4 Mr. and Mrs. Weasley and Ginny Weasley
Mrs. Weasley, despite all of her help to Harry and warnings to her children not to stare at him and embarrass him, surely must have been dying to get home and tell her husband about their encounter with the famous Harry Potter. ***Have Mr. and Mrs. Weasley and Ginny discuss the day's events over dinner.***

Scenario #5 Harry, Hagrid, and the Dursleys
Even though in the book Harry agreed readily to go into wizard training, imagine what might have happened had he refused. He would have had some reasons for his decision, Hagrid would have been obliged to convince him to go, and the Dursleys–all three of them–would have had their own points of view. ***Have Harry refuse emphatically to take Hogwarts up on their offer. Give Hagrid and the Dursleys ample time to argue their points of view.***

Lesson Fourteen

Objectives
1. To review Chapter Eight
2. To do the preview work for Chapters Nine and Ten: study questions and vocabulary
3. To read Chapters Nine and Ten in class
4. To have students give oral reports on the nonfiction reading assignment

Activity #1
Briefly review Chapter Eight.

Activity #2
Do the preview work for Chapters Nine and Ten as a class: short answer and vocabulary
You might mention to students that they will be asked to do longer reading assignments from here on in so it is imperative that they pay special attention to previewing and to the actual reading.

Activity #3
Read Chapters Nine and Ten in class.

Activity #4
Allow students a brief time to give oral reports on their nonfiction reading.

Lesson Fifteen

Objectives
1. To continue oral reports on the nonfiction reading assignment
2. To review Chapters Nine and Ten

Activity #1
Allow students to continue to give brief oral reports on their nonfiction reading.

Activity #2
Review the main events, ideas, and characterizations in Chapters Nine and Ten. At this point in the unit, the reviews are largely done just to give students the opportunity to ask any questions they may have and for you to help to avoid having any students slack off on their reading at this crucial juncture.

Lesson Sixteen

Objectives
1. To do the preview work on Chapters Eleven and Twelve: study questions and vocabulary
2. To give students the opportunity to write from personal opinion

Activity #1
Do the preview work on Chapters Eleven and Twelve: short answer and vocabulary.

Activity #2
Catch up on any loose ends. Think about whether or not you need to give a quiz, answer students' questions, follow up on any leftover odds and ends from previous lessons, etc.

Lesson Seventeen

Objectives
1. To read Chapters Eleven and Twelve
2. To do the preview work on Chapters Thirteen and Fourteen: short answer and vocabulary
3. To assign Chapters Thirteen and Fourteen to be read at home
4. To give students the opportunity to report on their projects

Activity #1
Have students read Chapters Eleven and Twelve out loud.

Activity #2
Do the preview work on Chapters Thirteen and Fourteen as a class: short answer and vocabulary

Activity #3
Assign Chapters Thirteen and Fourteen to be read at home. Remind students of the benefits of their reading out loud to someone at home.

Activity #4
Have students report on their projects. Because of time restraints, students should be encouraged to be brief–a few minutes per student will have to suffice.

Lesson Eighteen

Objectives
1.   To do the preview work for Chapters Fifteen and Sixteen: study questions and vocabulary.
2.   To assign Chapters Fifteen and Sixteen to be read at home
3.   To continue to allow students to report on their projects

Activity #1
Do the preview work for Chapters Fifteen and Sixteen: study questions and vocabulary.

Activity #2
Assign Chapters Fifteen and Sixteen to be read at home.

Activity #3
Continue to allow students to report briefly on their projects. If you have already given enough time to the projects, you might spend this time reading *part* of Chapters Fifteen and Sixteen during class time.

Lesson Nineteen

Objectives
1.   To do the preview work on Chapter Seventeen: study questions and vocabulary
2.   To finish reading **Harry Potter** in class, allowing time for any desirable discussion

Activity #1
Do the preview work on Chapter Seventeen: study questions and vocabulary.

Activity #2
Finish reading the book in class. This last chapter is extremely important. Feel free to linger over important events and statements, especially Dumbledore's explanations to Harry and Harry's reactions. You should have time to allow discussion to go on whenever necessary.

Lesson Twenty

Objectives
1. To review the whole book if such review is necessary
2. To allow students the opportunity to write from personal opinion

Activity #1
Spend as much time as you think you need on reviewing the whole book.

Activity #2
Make the personal opinion writing assignment. This should be a relatively easy assignment since it involves only an understanding of what students have read in **Harry Potter** and their personal thoughts about themselves and what they value.

If your class is advanced, you may find this writing assignment too simplistic. Given the possible range of levels of students reading the **Harry Potter** books, the assignment has been kept as reasonable as possible. You may, if you wish, go into some detail about myth and the archetypal hero and his or her search for an object or undertaking of a task and/or a journey–but you need not.

All students really need to understand for this writing assignment is that there was something that meant enough to Harry Potter (the Sorcerer's Stone) for him to go after it at great risk: the Sorcerer's Stone. The point of the assignment is for students to think about they might value enough to undertake a search for it, despite their own personal safety. The "thing" that they choose can be tangible or not. What really matters is that they think the issue through and express themselves clearly.

The directions for Writing Assignment #3 follow.

Writing Assignment #3 - Harry Potter
(Writing to Express a Personal Opinion)

PROMPT

In the reading you have done so far in **Harry Potter and the Sorcerer's Stone**, you have seen Harry and his friends willingly undertake risky missions in order to accomplish a particular goal. Listen to Harry as he explains his rationale for going after the Sorcerer's Stone:

> Don't you understand? If Snape gets hold of the Stone, Voldemort's coming back! Haven't you heard what it was like when he was trying to take over? There won't be any Hogwarts to get expelled from! He'll flatten it, or turn it into a school for the Dark Arts! Losing points doesn't matter anymore, can't you see? D'you think he'll leave you and your families alone if Gryffindor wins the house cup? If I get caught before I can get to the Stone, well, I'll have to go back to the Dursleys and wait for Voldemort to find me there, it's only dying a bit later than I would have, because I'm never going over to the Dark Side! I'm going through that trapdoor tonight and nothing you two say is going to stop me! Voldemort killed my parents, remember?

Your assignment is both extremely complex and extremely simple: you are to think about one thing (it can be tangible or intangible) that you value enough that you would be willing to risk everything you have to secure it. Then write a paper explaining what the thing is and why you would be willing to risk all for it.

PREWRITING

Choose your topic carefully and decide how you can explain something so important and personal. Think through how you can speak forcefully through the words you choose and the way you decide to present them.

DRAFTING

Write a draft in which you state your views as strongly and effectively as possible. Try to put yourself in the place of your potential reader. Make sure that you've explained everything thoroughly. Don't just assume that the reader will know what you mean. Avoid making statements like, "This means a lot to me." *Explain why*. Don't make circular arguments like, "It means a lot to me because it's so important." *Explain why*. You might want to explain by telling a story, by quoting someone famous, by referring to **Harry Potter**–whatever. Just make sure that you are explaining why you feel the way you do. This should be something that you feel passionate about: make the reader feel and understand your passion.

Writing Assignment #3 - **Harry Potter** - page 2

PROMPT

Because this is a personal piece of writing, you will not be asked to share it with your classmates. You are encouraged, however, to let someone you trust read it, just to see if you're making your point convincingly and effectively. No matter how good a piece of writing may be, it can *always* benefit from being critiqued by someone other than the author.

PROOFREADING

Proofread as carefully as you can. Try not to allow careless grammar, spelling, organization, and lack of clarity ruin an otherwise good piece of writing.

Lesson Twenty-One

<u>Objective</u>
    To do a vocabulary review for the whole book

<u>Activity</u>
You will be the best judge of how much vocabulary review your students need. However you choose to review, you may want to pick one or more of the vocabulary review activities listed on the next page and spend the class period as directed in the activity. Some additional materials for these review activities are located in the Vocabulary Resource Materials at the end of this unit.

Vocabulary Review Activities

1. Divide your class into two teams and have an old-fashioned spelling or definition bee.

2. Give each of your students (or students in groups of two, three, or four) a Vocabulary Word Search Puzzle based on **Harry Potter and the Sorcerer's Stone**. The person or group to find all of the vocabulary words in the puzzle first wins.

3. Give students a **Harry Potter** Vocabulary Word Search Puzzle without the word list. The person or group to find the most vocabulary words in the puzzle wins.

4. Use a **Harry Potter** Vocabulary Crossword Puzzle. Put a puzzle onto a transparency on the overhead projector so everyone can see it and do the puzzle together as a class.

5. Give students a **Harry Potter** Vocabulary Matching Worksheet to do.

6. Divide your class into two teams. Use **Harry Potter** vocabulary words with their letters jumbled as a word list. Student 1 from Team A faces off against Student 1 from Team B. You write the first jumbled word on the board. The first student (1A or 1B) to unscramble the word wins the chance for his or her team to score points. If 1A wins the jumble, go to 2A and give him or her a definition. He or she must give you the correct spelling of the vocabulary word which fits that definition. If he or she does, Team A scores a point, and you give 3A a definition for which you expect a correctly spelled matching vocabulary word. Continue giving Team A definitions until some team member makes an incorrect response. An incorrect response sends the game back to the jumbled-word face-off, this time with students 2A and 2B. Instead of repeating giving definitions to the first few students of each team, continue with the student after the one who gave the last incorrect response on the team. For example, if Team B wins the jumbled-word face-off and student 5B gave the last incorrect answer for Team B, you would start this round of definition questions with student 6B and so on. The team with the most points wins!

7. Have students write a story in which they correctly use as many vocabulary words as possible. Have students read their compositions orally. Post the most original compositions on your bulletin board.

UNIT TESTS

Short Answer Unit Test #1 - Harry Potter

I. Matching/Identify

___	Hermione Granger	A.	Headmaster of Hogwarts School
___	Ron Weasley	B.	Keeper of the Keys
___	Scabbers	C.	Harry's aunt
___	Professor Snape	D.	Harry's student rival
___	Rubeus Hagrid	E.	Girl who applies logic
___	Professor Dumbledore	F.	Ron's rat
___	Draco Malfoy	G.	Harry's close red-haired friend
___	Petunia Dursley	H.	Master of Potions

II. Short Answer

1. What big secret did Mr. and Mrs. Dursley want to keep?

2. What did Harry Potter's scar look like?

3. Why did Mr. and Mrs. Dursley move Harry into a different bedroom?

4. What was Gringotts?

5. From what platform did Harry's train to Hogwarts leave?

6. When was a Quidditch match over?

7. What was the Sorcerer's Stone said to be able to do?

Short Answer Unit Test #1 - **Harry Potter** - page 2

8. What was Hagrid looking up in the library?

9. Who was Quirrell's master?

10. What ultimately happened to the Sorcerer's Stone?

III. Essay
Explain the significance of at least three of the book's chapter titles.
Be specific and give details to explain the points you want to make.

Short Answer Unit Test #1 - **Harry Potter** - page 3

IV. Vocabulary
Listen to the vocabulary words and write them down. After you have spelled all the words, go back and write down the definitions.

1.

2.

3.

4.

5.

6.

7.

8.

9.

10.

Key - Short Answer Unit Test #1 - Harry Potter

I. Matching/Identify

E	Hermione Granger	A.	Headmaster of Hogwarts School
G	Ron Weasley	B.	Keeper of the Keys
F	Scabbers	C.	Harry's aunt
H	Professor Snape	D.	Harry's student rival
B	Rubeus Hagrid	E.	Girl who applies logic
A	Professor Dumbledore	F.	Ron's rat
D	Draco Malfoy	G.	Harry's close red-haired friend
C	Petunia Dursley	H.	Master of Potions

II. Short Answer

1. What big secret did Mr. and Mrs. Dursley want to keep?
   That they were related to Mrs. Dursley's sister

2. What did Harry Potter's scar look like?
   A lightning bolt

3. Why did Mr. and Mrs. Dursley move Harry into a different bedroom?
   Because the people who wrote Harry letters knew he slept in a cupboard under the stairs

4. What was Gringotts?
   A wizard bank

5. From what platform did Harry's train to Hogwarts leave?
   Platform Nine and Three-quarters

6. When was a Quidditch match over?
   When one team's Seeker caught the Golden Snitch

Key - Short Answer Unit Test #1 - **Harry Potter** - page 2

7. What was the Sorcerer's Stone said to be able to do?
   The Stone gave all the money a person could want and immortal life.

8. What was Hagrid looking up in the library?
   He was looking up information about dragons and their care.

9. Who was Quirrell's master?
   Voldemort

10. What ultimately happened to the Sorcerer's Stone?
    The Stone ultimately was destroyed.

III. Essay
   Explain the significance of at least three of the book's chapter titles.
   Be specific and give details to explain the points you want to make.
       You may want to make some notes here as to what answers you expect.

IV. Vocabulary
   Choose ten of the vocabulary words to dictate to your students.
   Write them here if you choose.

Short Answer Unit Test #2 - Harry Potter

I. Matching

____	Professor Snape	A.	Headmaster of Hogwarts School
____	Scabbers	B.	Harry's student rival
____	Hermione Granger	C.	Harry's aunt
____	Ron Weasley	D.	Keeper of the Keys
____	Rubeus Hagrid	E.	Girl who applies logic
____	Professor Dumbledore	F.	Master of Potions
____	Petunia Dursley	G.	Harry's close red-haired friend
____	Draco Malfoy	H.	Ron's rat

II. Short Answer

1. What was the first rule for a quiet life with the Dursleys?

2. What about Harry's second letter convinced Mr. Dursley that someone was watching the family?

3. What were Muggles?

4. Who was Voldemort?

5. What came inside the Chocolate Frogs that Harry bought?

6. What were the names of the four houses at Hogwarts School?

Short Answer Unit Test #2 - **Harry Potter** - page 2

7. How did Harry decide to test the invisibility cloak?

8. What were the students supposed to find in the forest?

9. Why had Professor Snape tried to protect Harry?

10. Which student was most surprised at being awarded points?

III. Quotations: Identify the speaker and explain the significance of these quotes.
1. "Er — Petunia, dear — you haven't heard from your sister lately, have you?"

2. "To Harry Potter — the boy who lived!"

3. "....It just so happens that the phoenix whose tail feather is in your wand, gave another feather — just one other. It is very curious indeed that you should be destined for this wand when its brother — why, its brother gave you that scar."

4. "His name's Scabbers and he's useless, he hardly ever wakes up. Percy got an owl from my dad for being made a prefect, but they couldn't aff — I mean, I got Scabbers instead."

5. "Potter, this is Oliver Wood. Wood — I've found you a Seeker."

Short Answer Unit Test #2 - **Harry Potter** - page 3

6. "You're saying it wrong....It's Wing-*gar*-dium Levi-*o*-sa, make the 'gar' nice and long."

7. "Yes..." said Ron softly, "it's the only way ... I've got to be taken."

8. "Well — yeah — how many three-headed dogs d'yeh meet, even around Hogwarts? So I told him, Fluffy's a piece of cake if yeh know how to calm him down, jus' play him a bit o' music an' he'll go straight off ter sleep —"

9. "....You see, only one who wanted to *find* the Stone — find it, but not use it — would be able to get it, otherwise they'd just see themselves making gold or drinking Elixir of Life...."

10. "There are all kinds of courage,"...."It takes a great deal of bravery to stand up to our enemies, but just as much to stand up to our friends."

Short Answer Unit Test #2 - **Harry Potter** - page 4

IV. Vocabulary

Listen to the vocabulary words and write them down. After you have spelled all the words, go back and write down the definitions.

1.

2.

3.

4.

5.

6.

7.

8.

9.

10.

Key - Short Answer Unit Test #2 - Harry Potter

I. Matching

F	Professor Snape	A.	Headmaster of Hogwarts School
H	Scabbers	B.	Harry's student rival
E	Hermione Granger	C.	Harry's aunt
G	Ron Weasley	D.	Keeper of the Keys
D	Rubeus Hagrid	E.	Girl who applies logic
A	Professor Dumbledore	F.	Master of Potions
C	Petunia Dursley	G.	Harry's close red-haired friend
B	Draco Malfoy	H.	Ron's rat

II. Short Answer

1. What was the first rule for a quiet life with the Dursleys?
   Don't ask questions.

2. What about Harry's second letter convinced Mr. Dursley that someone was watching the family?
   The letter was addressed to Harry at The Smallest Bedroom, 4 Privet Drive.

3. What were Muggles?
   Nonmagical folk

4. Who was Voldemort?
   The bad wizard who killed Harry's parents and tried to kill him.

5. What came inside the Chocolate Frogs that Harry bought?
   Collecting/trading cards

6. What were the names of the four houses at Hogwarts School?
   Gryffindor, Hufflepuff, Ravenclaw, and Slytherin

Key - Short Answer Unit Test #2 - **Harry Potter** - page 2

7. How did Harry decide to test the invisibility cloak?
   He decided to test it by wearing it and trying to get into the Restricted Section of the library.

8. What were the students supposed to find in the forest?
   A wounded unicorn

9. Why had Professor Snape tried to protect Harry?
   Because he hated Harry's father. He wanted to try to protect Harry so that he would be even with his father and could go back to hating him.

10. Which student was most surprised at being awarded points?
    Neville Longbottom

III. Quotations: Identify the speaker and explain the significance of these quotes.
1. "Er — Petunia, dear — you haven't heard from your sister lately, have you?"
   Mr. Dursley - very tentatively asking his wife about the strangely dressed people who he had seen that morning - he knew his wife would be upset at the mere mention of her sister.

2. "To Harry Potter — the boy who lived!"
   The wizards - they were celebrating that Harry had survived Lord Voldemort's attack on him.

3. "....It just so happens that the phoenix whose tail feather is in your wand, gave another feather — just one other. It is very curious indeed that you should be destined for this wand when its brother — why, its brother gave you that scar."
   Mr. Ollivander - the same phoenix gave a tail feather to both Harry's and Vandemort's wands.

4. "His name's Scabbers and he's useless, he hardly ever wakes up. Percy got an owl from my dad for being made a prefect, but they couldn't aff — I mean, I got Scabbers instead."
   Ron Weasley - very sensitive to coming from a financially strapped family - usually he keeps all things financial to himself.

5. "Potter, this is Oliver Wood. Wood — I've found you a Seeker."
   Professor McGonagall - she has seen Harry fly, and she is happy that Harry can now be the Seeker for the Gryffindor team.

Key - Short Answer Unit Test #2 - **Harry Potter** - page 3

6. "You're saying it wrong....It's Wing-*gar*-dium Levi-*o*-sa, make the 'gar' nice and long."
    Hermione Granger - Hermione is correcting Ron - she is very particular about being right.

7. "Yes....it's the only way ... I've got to be taken."
    Ron Weasley - explaining how he has to be sacrificed on the chess board so that he and Harry and Hermione can win the chess game and get to the other side of the room.

8. "Well — yeah — how many three-headed dogs d'yeh meet, even around Hogwarts? So I told him, Fluffy's a piece of cake if yeh know how to calm him down, jus' play him a bit o' music an' he'll go straight off ter sleep —"
    Hagrid - suddenly he realizes that he has given away to a stranger in the bar the terrible secret that could cost a great deal.

9. "....You see, only one who wanted to *find* the Stone — find it, but not use it — would be able to get it, otherwise they'd just see themselves making gold or drinking Elixir of Life...."
    Professor Dumbledore - explaining why the purity of the desire presented by Harry is what gained him the Stone.

10. "There are all kinds of courage,"...."It takes a great deal of bravery to stand up to our enemies, but just as much to stand up to our friends."
    Professor Dumbledore - awarding points to Neville Longbottom for standing up to Hermione and Harry

IV. Vocabulary
    Choose ten words to dictate to your students. Write them here if you wish.

Advanced Short Answer Unit Test - Harry Potter

I. Matching

____	Professor Sprout	A.	Three-headed guard dog
____	Professor Quirrell's course	B.	Harry's new broomstick
____	Lily Potter	C.	Herbology professor
____	Mrs. Figg	D.	Headmaster of Hogwarts School
____	New Nimbus Two thousand	E.	Creator of the Sorcerer's Stone
____	Fluffy	F.	Defense Against the Dark Arts
____	Nicolas Flamel	G.	Harry's mother
____	Professor Dumbledore	H.	Mad old lady who lived near the Dursleys

II. Short Answer

1. Show as clearly as you can the ways in which Harry Potter's character develops throughout the book. Be sure to use specific examples from the text.

2. Why did the Sorcerer's Stone have to be destroyed?

3. Who is responsible for the Sorcerer's Stone having caused problems? Explain your answer as fully as possible.

Advanced Short Answer Unit Test - **Harry Potter** - page 2

4. Explain Professor Snape's reasons for trying to protect Harry? Were there other ways that he could have repaid his debt to the past and continued to carry his hatred with him?

5. Did Ron need to sacrifice himself temporarily in the chess game? Explain.

III. Quotations: Explain the meaning and importance to the story of the following quotations.

1. "Er — Petunia, dear — you haven't heard from your sister lately, have you?"

2. "They stuff people's heads down the toilet the first day at Stonewall," he told Harry.

3. "All you have to do is walk straight at the barrier between platforms nine and ten. Don't stop and don't be scared you'll crash into it, that's very important...."

4. "HAVE YOU GONE MAD?"...."ARE YOU A WITCH OR NOT?"

5. "Your mother died to save you. If there's one thing Voldemort cannot understand, it is love...."

Advanced Short Answer Unit Test - **Harry Potter** - page 3

6. "....You see, only one who wanted to *find* the Stone — find it, but not use it — would be able to get it, otherwise they'd just see themselves making gold or drinking Elixir of Life...."

7. "You're saying it wrong....It's Wing-*gar*-dium Levi-*o*-sa, make the 'gar' nice and long."

IV. Vocabulary
Listen to the vocabulary words and write them down. After you have written down all the words, write a paragraph in which you use all the words. The paragraph must in some way relate to **Harry Potter and the Sorcerer's Stone**.

Unit Test - Harry Potter
Multiple Choice - Matching #1

I. Matching

____ 1. Hermione Granger   A. Headmaster of Hogwarts School

____ 2. Ron Weasley   B. Keeper of the Keys

____ 3. Scabbers   C. Harry's aunt

____ 4. Professor Snape   D. Harry's student rival

____ 5. Rubeus Hagrid   E. Girl who applies logic

____ 6. Professor Dumbledore   F. Ron's rat

____ 7. Draco Malfoy   G. Harry's close red-haired friend

____ 8. Petunia Dursley   H. Master of Potions

II. Multiple Choice

1. What did Mr. Dursley do for a living?
    a. He was a big-time politician.
    b. He was a fireman.
    c. He was the director of Grunnings, a firm which made drills.
    d. He was the supervisor of a plastics manufacturing firm.

2. What was the first unusual thing that Mr. Dursley thought he saw as he left for work?
    a. He thought he saw a dog chasing its tail.
    b. He thought he saw a storm coming up.
    c. He thought he saw a cat reading a map.
    d. He thought he saw Harry Potter crossing the street ahead of him.

3. Why was Albus Dumbledore in the Dursleys' neighborhood?
    a. He had heard about the beauty of Privet Drive.
    b. He was doing a survey of the neighborhood.
    c. He had come to ask that Harry become a junior wizard.
    d. He had come to bring Harry Potter to his aunt and uncle.

Unit Test - MC#1 - **Harry Potter** - page 2

4. What was the first rule for a quiet life with the Dursleys?
   - a.. Don't make waves.
   - b. Don't ever cry.
   - c. Don't ask questions.
   - d. Don't sass adults.

5. What were Muggles?
   - a. Nonmagic folk
   - b. People who lived in the town
   - c. Old people
   - d. Stupid folk

6. Why did everyone at the train station stare at and want to meet Harry?
   - a. Because he was the only boy not dressed in a robe
   - b. Because he was famous and they had already heard of him
   - c. Because he was one of the shortest boys there
   - d. Because he was very good looking and smart

7. Why didn't Ron buy anything to eat on the train?
   - a. He knew the food was really bad.
   - b. He wasn't a bit hungry.
   - c. He hated train food.
   - d. He didn't buy anything because he couldn't afford to.

8. What were the four words Professor Dumbledore spoke before the banquet at Hogwarts?
   - a. Courage, loyalty, fidelity, and strength
   - b. Nitwit! Blubber! Oddment! Tweak!
   - c. Onward! Upward! Forward! Scoring!
   - d. Quidditch, Scores, Snitching, Seeking

9. Who was the Hogwarts caretaker?
   - a. Hagrid
   - b. Mr. Filch
   - c. Mrs. Norris
   - d. Albus Dumbledore

Unit Test - MC#1 - **Harry Potter** - page 3

10. Who gave away the secret of how to get past Fluffy?
    a. Hermione
    b. Nicolas Flamel
    c. Snape
    d. Hagrid

III. Essay

It is said that there are many important lessons that readers can learn in **Harry Potter and the Sorcerer's Stone**. Isolate at least three such lessons, show how they are demonstrated in the book, and explain why they are important.

Unit Test - MC#1 - **Harry Potter** - page 4

IV.   Vocabulary (Matching)

1.	shuddered	A.	snickered
2.	spectacles	B.	delayed leaving
3.	sniggered	C.	moving gently
4.	tufts	D.	image
5.	enormous	E.	certain
6.	expelled	F.	partially open
7.	savaging	G.	turned suddenly
8.	rubbish	H.	delay
9.	lingered	I.	glasses
10.	destiny	J.	shivered, as from fear or aversion
11.	scowl	K.	short strands of hair
12.	wafting	L.	very big
13.	mangled	M.	attacking violently
14.	reflection	N.	garbage, trash
15.	biased	O.	delayed leaving
16.	hitch	P.	frown angrily
17.	convinced	Q.	torn, mutilated
18.	omen	R.	prejudiced
19.	ajar	S.	sign
20.	wheeled	T.	forced, put out

Unit Test - Harry Potter
Multiple Choice - Matching #2

I. Matching

____ 1. Professor Snape A. Headmaster of Hogwarts School

____ 2. Scabbers B. Harry's student rival

____ 3. Hermione Granger C. Harry's aunt

____ 4. Ron Weasley D. Keeper of the Keys

____ 5. Rubeus Hagrid E. Girl who applies logic

____ 6. Professor Dumbledore F. Master of Potions

____ 7. Petunia Dursley G. Harry's close red-haired friend

____ 8. Draco Malfoy H. Ron's rat

II. Multiple Choice

1. What person suddenly appeared next to the cat?
    a. Draco Malfoy
    b. Dudley Dursley
    c. Hermione Granger
    d. Albus Dumbledore

2. What did Harry Potter's scar look like?
    a. His scar looked like a miniature goblin.
    b. His scar looked like a big birthmark.
    c. His scar looked like a large cat.
    d. His scar looked like a bolt of lightning.

3. Who got all of the good things in the Dursley household?
    a. Dudley Dursley, Harry's cousin
    b. Harry's owl
    c. Mrs. Dursley
    d. Harry

Unit Test - MC#2 - **Harry Potter** - page 2

4. What was Dudley's favorite sport?
   a. It was soccer.
   b. It was Quidditch.
   c. It was Harry Hunting.
   d. It was basketball.

5. What strange thing happened at the hotel?
   a. Everyone stared at Harry.
   b. Mrs. Dursley had too much to drink in the bar.
   c. Hundreds of letters arrived addressed to Harry in Room 17 of the Railview Hotel.
   d. More than thirty letters arrived addressed to The Traveling Dursley Family.

6. Who was Voldemort?
   a. He was Mrs. Dursley's grandfather.
   b. He was a troll.
   c. He was descended from a goblin.
   d. He was a wizard gone bad.

7. How did Hagrid get to the shack in the middle of the water?
   a. He flew there.
   b. He rented a boat on the other shore.
   c. He was rowed across by a friendly goblin.
   d. He walked across the water.

8. What was Professor Quirrell's most notable trait?
   a. He stuttered.
   b. He laughed a lot.
   c. His nice smile
   d. His beard

9. What was the name of Harry's owl?
   a. Norbert
   b. Hedwig
   c. Scabbers
   d. Hermione

Unit Test - MC#2 - **Harry Potter** - page 3

10. What were the names of the four houses at Hogwarts?
    a. Dopey, Sneezy, Harry, and Griffin
    b. Gryffindor, Hufflepuff, Ravenclaw, and Slytherin
    c. Slytherin, Ravenclaw, HuffandPuff, and Nod
    d. Hermione, Ron, George, and Fred

III. Essay
Explain the reason for the names of at least three (3) of the chapters in **Harry Potter and the Sorcerer's Stone**. Then explain briefly the importance of the chapter to the book overall. The chapter names are listed below.

The Boy Who Lived	The Midnight Duel
The Vanishing Glass	Halloween
The Letters from No One	Quidditch
The Keeper of the Keys	The Mirror of Erised
Diagon Alley	Nicolas Flamel
The Journey from Platform Nine and Three-quarters	
The Sorting Hat	Norbert the Norwegian Ridgeback
The Potions Master	The Forbidden Forest
Through the Trapdoor	The Man with Two Faces

Unit Test - MC#2 - **Harry Potter** - page 4

IV. Vocabulary (Matching)

1.	shuddered	A.	partially open
2.	spectacles	B.	delayed leaving
3.	sniggered	C.	moving gently
4.	tufts	D.	short strands of hair
5.	enormous	E.	very big
6.	expelled	F.	snickered
7.	savaging	G.	turned suddenly
8.	rubbish	H.	delay
9.	lingered	I.	glasses
10.	destiny	J.	shivered, as from fear or aversion
11.	scowl	K.	image
12.	wafting	L.	certain
13.	mangled	M.	attacking violently
14.	reflection	N.	sign
15.	biased	O.	delayed leaving
16.	hitch	P.	frown angrily
17.	convinced	Q.	torn, mutilated
18.	omen	R.	forced, put out
19.	ajar	S.	garbage, trash
20.	wheeled	T.	prejudiced

Multiple Choice Answer Sheet - Harry Potter

I. Matching	II. Multiple Choice	IV. Vocabulary	
1. _____	1. _____	1. _____	11. _____
2. _____	2. _____	2. _____	12. _____
3. _____	3. _____	3. _____	13. _____
4. _____	4. _____	4. _____	14. _____
5. _____	5. _____	5. _____	15. _____
6. _____	6. _____	6. _____	16. _____
7. _____	7. _____	7. _____	17. _____
8. _____	8. _____	8. _____	18. _____
	9. _____	9. _____	19. _____
	10. _____	10. _____	20. _____

III. Essay: Write your response to the essay question here. Use the back of this page if necessary.

Multiple Choice Answer Key - Harry Potter

Answers for Test 1 are in the left-hand columns. Answers for Test 2 are in the right-hand columns.

I. Matching		II. Multiple Choice		IV. Vocabulary			
1. E	F	1. c	d	1. J	J	11. P	P
2. G	H	2. c	d	2. I	I	12. C	C
3. F	E	3. d	a	3. A	F	13. Q	Q
4. H	G	4. c	c	4. K	D	14. D	K
5. B	D	5. a	c	5. L	E	15. R	T
6. A	A	6. b	d	6. T	R	16. H	H
7. D	C	7. d	a	7. M	M	17. E	L
8. C	B	8. b	a	8. N	S	18. S	N
		9. b	b	9. B	B	19. F	A
		10. d	b	10. O	O	20. G	G

UNIT RESOURCE MATERIALS

Bulletin Board Ideas - Harry Potter

1. See the bulletin board activity in Lesson One.

2. Get students to cut out pictures from magazines and newspapers that demonstrate belonging–to a group, to a class, with others who believe as one does.

   Perhaps they can find pictures of groups of people sharing activities. But you should also try to get them to find pictures that show some people on the fringes of a group. Show how it might *look* to be apart from a group.

   Certainly being alone some of the time isn't bad or wrong–it is, however, uncomfortable and makes one sad if one is not alone by choice.

   Discuss briefly how it feels to be *with* a group but not be *part* of that group. See if students would like to discuss being excluded simply because one is not liked or doesn't fit in.

3. Do a bulletin board activity about magic. It might be very easy to find pictures of the Harry Potter phenomenon. There surely will continue to be pictures of Harry Potter and others from the books as well as likenesses and suggestions of Potter in much advertising. Perhaps students can cut out advertisements and suggest ways to incorporate Harry Potterisms into it.

   If nothing else, you might be able to copy a few pictures from the Internet to put on your bulletin board. The whole idea is simply to generate and maintain interest in the book.

4. Sometimes it can be interesting to write down some of the lines spoken by characters in the novel and affix them to the bulletin board or write them on the chalk board. Or there might be ordinary pictures put on the board with "talking balloons" suggesting what they may be saying: two people together, for instance, doing something risky, and one of them is shouting, "HAVE YOU GONE MAD? ARE YOU A WITCH OR NOT?" Or two people together and one is saying to the other, "Ah, shut up, yeh great prune."

5. If students like **Harry Potter and the Sorcerer's Stone**, they might write fan mail to the author, J. K. Rowling, and post the half dozen best results on the board. With some luck, they might actually get responses from the author or her agents.

6. Have students write letters to local newspapers regarding the book and explaining why it is good or not. Not only might you post the letters on the classroom bulletin board, but it is possible that some students could actually get their letters published.

Bulletin Board Ideas - **Harry Potter** - page 2

7. Students might try their hands at writing letters pretending to be from one **Harry Potter** character to another. From Harry to Hermione: "Dear Hermione, I'm back on Privet Drive for the holidays. Nothing much has changed except that Dudley has gotten even fatter...."

   And Hermione could write back, "Dear Harry, so you think you've got it back this Christmas–how would you like to live with a couple of parents who debate the virtues of dental flossing day and night?" Or Professor Dumbledore leaving a note for the students: "Nitwit! Blubber! Oddment! Tweak!" These are, of course, just-for-fun activities that might help to keep interest in the novel high. Students might enjoy seeing their handiwork posted on the bulletin board from time to time.

8. You might significantly enlarge a word search puzzle and post it on the bulletin board. Invite students to take their pens or markers and find the words before and/or after class, or perhaps this could be a useful activity for students who finish their work early.

Extra Activities - Harry Potter

One of the difficulties in teaching a novel is that not all students read at the same speed. One student who likes to read may take the book home and finish it in a day or two. Sometimes a few students finish the in-class assignments early. The problem, then, is finding suitable extra activities for students.

One thing that helps with this problem is to keep a little library in the classroom. For this unit on **Harry Potter**, you might check out from the school library other Young Adult books. You might try to have on hand some of the other **Harry Potter** books for eager readers. These books can be obtained for relatively little cost, so you might like to have one of each of the series all during the unit. You might also be able to bring some of the books from the library to the classroom.

A biography of the author would be interesting for some students. You may include other related books and articles that focus on some aspect of magic, making movies out of books, etc. Students could check best-seller book lists weekly to chart the success of the Potter books.

Other things you may keep on hand are puzzles. Some puzzles relating directly to **Harry Potter** follow this page in your LitPlan.

Some students may like to draw, to sing, to dance, to paint, or participate in some other artistic endeavor. You might devise a contest or allow some extra-credit grade for your more artistic students. Note, too, that whatever students present might be used as bulletin board materials in the future. Check to see if students prefer to keep their artistic work; many will be persuaded to participate because they like the "immortality" they will achieve with future classes of students who use their classroom.

The pages which follow contain games, puzzles, and worksheets. The keys, when appropriate, immediately follow the puzzle or worksheet. There are two main groups of activities: one group for the unit; that is, generally relating to the **Harry Potter** text, and another group of activities related strictly to **Harry Potter** vocabulary.

Directions for the games, puzzles, and worksheets are self-explanatory. The object here is to provide you with extra materials you may use in any way you choose.

More Activities - Harry Potter

1. Have students write a brief epilogue to **Harry Potter and the Sorcerer's Stone.** Harry could, for example, wake up as from a dream only to find that he simply imagined the whole Hogwarts episode.

2. Have students think about what **Harry Potter and the Sorcerer's Stone** might be like if Harry Potter were female instead of male. How would Hogwarts seem different if girls were the heroes of the book instead of, for the most part. Suppose the book under discussion were called **Hillary Potter and the Sorcerer's Stone**.

3. Have students do a brief writeup on what each of the first-year students might be doing professionally as adults.

4. If you have students who are artistically talented, you might have them write a short musical piece, write a song, or choreograph a dance sequence based on one episode/aspect of **Harry Potter.** The artistic rendering could then be performed for the whole class.

5. Have students write "customer reviews" like the ones that appear on web sites for book sellers. The reviews need only be a paragraph or so long..

6. Have students discuss and then write briefly about what they would do were they to suddenly have Harry's powers. What would they do with that kind of power?

7. Have students write an obituary for Voldemort. Have students report his death in the style of a major television commentator. How about having Voldemort appear on the Oprah show or 60 Minutes?

8. Assume that Voldemort has been arrested for killing Harry Potter's parents. How would he be charged? What would the media say about him? Would the county or city be able to assemble a jury of *his* peers? Think of having a kind of mock trial to consider the charges against Voldemort.

9. Ask students to think about which character in **Harry Potter** they most identify with. Have students get up in front of the class and tell the class about themselves in the role of the character they have chosen.

More Activities - **Harry Potter** - page 2

10. Pick any character in the book and place him or her on a television show like Letterman or Leno. Think about the types of questions that might be asked.

11. Do a mock Who Wants to be a Millionaire show with the characters as guests. Who might be the most successful of the characters.

12. Have students think of having one of the young characters become a student in your school. Do they think the person would be accepted? Would he or she be popular?
    Turn the exercise around and picture one of the professors in the book as a teacher at your school.

13. Have each student learn a "magic" trick and perform it for the class.

14. Show the movie **Harry Potter And The Sorcerer's Stone** and have students compare and contrast it with the book.

15. Print out a list of web sites relating to Harry Potter. Assign each student one web site to explore. Students should print out any particularly interesting pages from the site and be able to explain what is on the site. You could take this a step further and have students get together in small groups to compare/contrast the sites they explored. You could even take it a step further and have students design (on paper) a Harry Potter web site combining all the best elements from all the web sites they viewed, plus their own ideas.

WORD LIST HARRY POTTER

No.	Word	Clue/Definition
1.	HEDWIG	Harry's owl
2.	VERNON	Harry's uncle
3.	HAGRID	Keeper of the Keys
4.	WEASLEY	Harry's close, red-haired friend
5.	SEEKER	Harry's role in Quidditch
6.	FILCH	Caretaker of Hogwarts
7.	NORRIS	Mr. Filch's cat
8.	DENTISTS	Hermione's parents' profession
9.	HAT	The Sorting____; assigns students to houses at Hogwarts
10.	JORDAN	Did commentary for the Quidditch match
11.	HERMIONE	Girl who applies logic
12.	LILY	Harry's mother
13.	SCABBERS	Ron's rat
14.	SLYTHERIN	Voldemort's house at Hogwarts
15.	INVISIBILITY	Just In Case note was left on the ___ cloak
16.	GRYFFINDOR	Harry's house at Hogwarts
17.	TWINS	Fred and George were ____
18.	ROWLING	Author of the Harry Potter books
19.	JAMES	Harry's father
20.	AGES	Quidditch Through The ____; book Hermione lent Harry
21.	FLUFFY	Three-headed dog
22.	BARON	The Bloody____; Slytherin ghost
23.	SPROUT	Herbology professor
24.	MALFOY	Harry's student rival
25.	FOREST	Place off-limits to students; Forbidden____
26.	DARK	Quirrell's course; Defense Against the ____ Arts
27.	SNITCH	Ball the Seeker had to catch; The Golden____
28.	GRINGOTTS	Wizard bank
29.	MUGGLES	Nonmagic fold
30.	DUMBLEDORE	Headmaster of Hogwarts School
31.	SNAPE	Master of Potions
32.	VOLDEMORT	Wizard gone bad
33.	PETUNIA	Harry's aunt
34.	TREVOR	Neville's toad
35.	PERCY	Prefect at Hogwarts;____Weasley
36.	OLLIVANDER	Seller of wands
37.	NEVILLE	____Longbottom; won points for standing up to his friends
38.	DUDLEY	Harry's cousin
39.	HOGWARTS	School of Witchcraft and Wizardry
40.	QUIDDITCH	Wizard game
41.	NICK	Nearly Headless____; resident ghost at Gryffindor House
42.	PEEVES	A poltergeist
43.	FANG	Hagrid's dog

WORD SEARCH - HARRY POTTER

```
N E V I L L E K Q E Y E L S A E W Z S Y
M Y L N J P D T R L P R R L P T X E F S
A M J V O F U O I N G E V Y S R M H Y J
L W N I G L D L K L B F E T F A O T M N
F V J S X E L T G B L M R H J H D U K Q
O H T I L X E I A G R Q N E V O E N T G
Y R X B S L Y C V C O F O R O G N Y F P
F M M I D B S W J A D X N I L W T H L R
M U H L F O R E S T N D N N D A I M U Z
D X S I Y Y B Z L K I D D Y E R S X F C
C V T T H B Z J R F F E E P M T T G F T
L X T Y C S P Q O Z F N R R O S S P Y M
Q Z O D C G F W W Y Y O E J R D E X H V
G K G G W T H V L Q R I K F T E F Y Q Y
P V N N M W H Z I P G M E F V J B K G M
B E I K H I S A N K R R E E N F G A Z W
J O R D A N M U G G L E S H C T I N S R
C V G C A S O N H E G H W F T N W L O M
P M Z P Y W A R N A S M T P U V D V C K
D G E H L F F O R N G J R T M S E V F H
Z A M A V B R N N I J R E K G R H R T Y
R H R T Z A F B R C S P I C T V Q W L X
N Z Q K B R R J Y K Q U I D D I T C H B
```

AGES	FOREST	JAMES	PEEVES	SNITCH
BARON	GRINGOTTS	JORDAN	PERCY	SPROUT
DARK	GRYFFINDOR	LILY	PETUNIA	TREVOR
DENTISTS	HAGRID	MALFOY	QUIDDITCH	TWINS
DUDLEY	HAT	MUGGLES	ROWLING	VERNON
DUMBLEDORE	HEDWIG	NEVILLE	SCABBERS	VOLDEMORT
FANG	HERMIONE	NICK	SEEKER	WEASLEY
FILCH	HOGWARTS	NORRIS	SLYTHERIN	
FLUFFY	INVISIBILITY	OLLIVANDER	SNAPE	

WORD SEARCH ANSWER KEY - HARRY POTTER

```
N E V I L L E     E Y E L S A E W   S
M     N     D R L     R L P       E
A     V O   U O I   E V Y   R M
L     I O L D L   B R T   A O D
F     S L E   I   B R H J H D U
O     I   E A V   R N V O E N   T
Y     B   Y C V   O O I G N   F
      M I   S   A D N I W T   L
  U   L   F O R E S T N   D A I   U
D     S I         D   E R S   S F
    T T         R   F O   M O   S F
      O Y       O   Y N   R   P Y
      G       T L   R I   T V
P     N       W I   G M   V E
  E   I     S A N   R E   F G A
J O R D A N M U G G L E S H C T I N S R
    R G C A S O N H E   H   N W L O
      P Y   A R N A S   U D V C
D   E H   F O R N G   T   E H
  A   A     R I   R E   R
    R T       A   S P I   T
      K B       K Q U I D D I T C H
```

AGES	FOREST	JAMES	PEEVES	SNITCH
BARON	GRINGOTTS	JORDAN	PERCY	SPROUT
DARK	GRYFFINDOR	LILY	PETUNIA	TREVOR
DENTISTS	HAGRID	MALFOY	QUIDDITCH	TWINS
DUDLEY	HAT	MUGGLES	ROWLING	VERNON
DUMBLEDORE	HEDWIG	NEVILLE	SCABBERS	VOLDEMORT
FANG	HERMIONE	NICK	SEEKER	WEASLEY
FILCH	HOGWARTS	NORRIS	SLYTHERIN	
FLUFFY	INVISIBILITY	OLLIVANDER	SNAPE	

CROSSWORD - HARRY POTTER

Across
- 3. Harry's owl
- 5. Fred and George were ____
- 7. Hagrid's dog
- 8. Nearly Headless____; resident ghost at Gryffindor House
- 9. Harry's mother
- 12. Prefect at Hogwarts;____Weasley
- 13. Harry's role in Quidditch
- 16. Quidditch Through The ____; book Hermione lent Harry
- 17. Mr. Filch's cat
- 18. Did commentary for the Quidditch match
- 19. Place off-limits to students; Forbidden____

Down
- 1. Harry's house at Hogwarts
- 2. Caretaker of Hogwarts
- 3. Keeper of the Keys
- 4. Hermione's parents' profession
- 6. Ball the Seeker had to catch; The Golden____
- 10. Girl who applies logic
- 11. Harry's uncle
- 14. The Sorting____; assigns students to houses at Hogwarts
- 15. Neville's toad

CROSSWORD ANSWER KEY - HARRY POTTER

Across
- 3. Harry's owl
- 5. Fred and George were ____
- 7. Hagrid's dog
- 8. Nearly Headless____; resident ghost at Gryffindor House
- 9. Harry's mother
- 12. Prefect at Hogwarts;____Weasley
- 13. Harry's role in Quidditch
- 16. Quidditch Through The ____; book Hermione lent Harry
- 17. Mr. Filch's cat
- 18. Did commentary for the Quidditch match
- 19. Place off-limits to students; Forbidden____

Down
- 1. Harry's house at Hogwarts
- 2. Caretaker of Hogwarts
- 3. Keeper of the Keys
- 4. Hermione's parents' profession
- 6. Ball the Seeker had to catch; The Golden____
- 10. Girl who applies logic
- 11. Harry's uncle
- 14. The Sorting____; assigns students to houses at Hogwarts
- 15. Neville's toad

MATCHING 1 - HARRY POTTER

___ 1. SNITCH   A. Ron's rat
___ 2. FANG   B. Neville's toad
___ 3. GRINGOTTS   C. Harry's owl
___ 4. JAMES   D. Did commentary for the Quidditch match
___ 5. FOREST   E. Wizard bank
___ 6. QUIDDITCH   F. Author of the Harry Potter books
___ 7. BARON   G. Keeper of the Keys
___ 8. HAT   H. Place off-limits to students; Forbidden____
___ 9. LILY   I. The Bloody____; Slytherin ghost
___ 10. NICK   J. Quirrell's course; Defense Against the ____ Arts
___ 11. HEDWIG   K. Headmaster of Hogwarts School
___ 12. SNAPE   L. Harry's aunt
___ 13. SCABBERS   M. Wizard game
___ 14. HAGRID   N. Ball the Seeker had to catch; The Golden____
___ 15. TREVOR   O. Harry's father
___ 16. ROWLING   P. The Sorting____; assigns students to houses at Hogwarts
___ 17. DARK   Q. Fred and George were ____
___ 18. PETUNIA   R. Girl who applies logic
___ 19. JORDAN   S. A poltergeist
___ 20. HERMIONE   T. Harry's mother
___ 21. WEASLEY   U. Master of Potions
___ 22. TWINS   V. Harry's close, red-haired friend
___ 23. DUDLEY   W. Hagrid's dog
___ 24. DUMBLEDORE   X. Nearly Headless____; resident ghost at Gryffindor House
___ 25. PEEVES   Y. Harry's cousin

MATCHING 1 ANSWER KEY - HARRY POTTER

N - 1.	SNITCH	A.	Ron's rat
W - 2.	FANG	B.	Neville's toad
E - 3.	GRINGOTTS	C.	Harry's owl
O - 4.	JAMES	D.	Did commentary for the Quidditch match
H - 5.	FOREST	E.	Wizard bank
M - 6.	QUIDDITCH	F.	Author of the Harry Potter books
I - 7.	BARON	G.	Keeper of the Keys
P - 8.	HAT	H.	Place off-limits to students; Forbidden____
T - 9.	LILY	I.	The Bloody____; Slytherin ghost
X - 10.	NICK	J.	Quirrell's course; Defense Against the ____ Arts
C - 11.	HEDWIG	K.	Headmaster of Hogwarts School
U - 12.	SNAPE	L.	Harry's aunt
A - 13.	SCABBERS	M.	Wizard game
G - 14.	HAGRID	N.	Ball the Seeker had to catch; The Golden____
B - 15.	TREVOR	O.	Harry's father
F - 16.	ROWLING	P.	The Sorting____; assigns students to houses at Hogwarts
J - 17.	DARK	Q.	Fred and George were ____
L - 18.	PETUNIA	R.	Girl who applies logic
D - 19.	JORDAN	S.	A poltergeist
R - 20.	HERMIONE	T.	Harry's mother
V - 21.	WEASLEY	U.	Master of Potions
Q - 22.	TWINS	V.	Harry's close, red-haired friend
Y - 23.	DUDLEY	W.	Hagrid's dog
K - 24.	DUMBLEDORE	X.	Nearly Headless____; resident ghost at Gryffindor House
S - 25.	PEEVES	Y.	Harry's cousin

MATCHING 2 - HARRY POTTER

___ 1. FLUFFY   A. Place off-limits to students; Forbidden____
___ 2. SNAPE   B. Neville's toad
___ 3. QUIDDITCH   C. Keeper of the Keys
___ 4. TREVOR   D. Harry's uncle
___ 5. HAGRID   E. Nearly Headless____; resident ghost at Gryffindor House
___ 6. GRYFFINDOR   F. Wizard game
___ 7. OLLIVANDER   G. Harry's house at Hogwarts
___ 8. SLYTHERIN   H. Master of Potions
___ 9. FOREST   I. Just In Case note was left on the ___ cloak
___10. INVISIBILITY   J. Seller of wands
___11. MUGGLES   K. Wizard gone bad
___12. VOLDEMORT   L. Three-headed dog
___13. PERCY   M. Nonmagic fold
___14. SCABBERS   N. Harry's cousin
___15. VERNON   O. Voldemort's house at Hogwarts
___16. JORDAN   P. Caretaker of Hogwarts
___17. NORRIS   Q. Herbology professor
___18. NICK   R. ____Longbottom; won points for standing up to his friends
___19. SPROUT   S. Harry's close, red-haired friend
___20. PETUNIA   T. Mr. Filch's cat
___21. NEVILLE   U. The Sorting____; assigns students to houses at Hogwarts
___22. DUDLEY   V. Harry's aunt
___23. HAT   W. Prefect at Hogwarts;____Weasley
___24. FILCH   X. Did commentary for the Quidditch match
___25. WEASLEY   Y. Ron's rat

MATCHING 2 ANSWER KEY - HARRY POTTER

L - 1.	FLUFFY	A. Place off-limits to students; Forbidden____
H - 2.	SNAPE	B. Neville's toad
F - 3.	QUIDDITCH	C. Keeper of the Keys
B - 4.	TREVOR	D. Harry's uncle
C - 5.	HAGRID	E. Nearly Headless____; resident ghost at Gryffindor House
G - 6.	GRYFFINDOR	F. Wizard game
J - 7.	OLLIVANDER	G. Harry's house at Hogwarts
O - 8.	SLYTHERIN	H. Master of Potions
A - 9.	FOREST	I. Just In Case note was left on the ___ cloak
I - 10.	INVISIBILITY	J. Seller of wands
M - 11.	MUGGLES	K. Wizard gone bad
K - 12.	VOLDEMORT	L. Three-headed dog
W - 13.	PERCY	M. Nonmagic fold
Y - 14.	SCABBERS	N. Harry's cousin
D - 15.	VERNON	O. Voldemort's house at Hogwarts
X - 16.	JORDAN	P. Caretaker of Hogwarts
T - 17.	NORRIS	Q. Herbology professor
E - 18.	NICK	R. ____Longbottom; won points for standing up to his friends
Q - 19.	SPROUT	S. Harry's close, red-haired friend
V - 20.	PETUNIA	T. Mr. Filch's cat
R - 21.	NEVILLE	U. The Sorting____; assigns students to houses at Hogwarts
N - 22.	DUDLEY	V. Harry's aunt
U - 23.	HAT	W. Prefect at Hogwarts; ____Weasley
P - 24.	FILCH	X. Did commentary for the Quidditch match
S - 25.	WEASLEY	Y. Ron's rat

JUGGLE LETTERS - HARRY POTTER

1. UTIPENA = 1. _____
Harry's aunt

2. RTINSEHYL = 2. _____
Voldemort's house at Hogwarts

3. EASG = 3. _____
Quidditch Through The ____; book Hermione lent Harry

4. EEVSPE = 4. _____
A poltergeist

5. UQTHCIDID = 5. _____
Wizard game

6. YRECP = 6. _____
Prefect at Hogwarts;____Weasley

7. ATH = 7. _____
The Sorting____; assigns students to houses at Hogwarts

8. YILL = 8. _____
Harry's mother

9. EEEKRS = 9. _____
Harry's role in Quidditch

10. AFNG =10. _____
Hagrid's dog

11. AESMJ =11. _____
Harry's father

12. SPENA =12. _____
Master of Potions

13. URPOTS =13. _____
Herbology professor

14. GGMUSLE =14. _____
Nonmagic fold

15. GDIHRA =15. _____
Keeper of the Keys

16. IVOAELRDNL =16. _____
Seller of wands

17. SLAEEWY =17. _____
Harry's close, red-haired friend

18. INCK =18. _____
Nearly Headless____; resident ghost at Gryffindor House

19. GSOGNTITR =19. _____
Wizard bank

20. CBSBARSE =20. _____
Ron's rat

21. ROESFT =21. _____
Place off-limits to students; Forbidden____

22. EHMNROEI =22. _____
Girl who applies logic

23. NTIWS =23. _____
Fred and George were ____

24. NOEVRN =24. _____
Harry's uncle

25. NJAODR =25. _____
Did commentary for the Quidditch match

26. HNSICT =26. _____
Ball the Seeker had to catch; The Golden____

27. SOINRR =27. _____
Mr. Filch's cat

28. OBARN =28. _____
The Bloody____; Slytherin ghost

29. LEUDYD =29. _____
Harry's cousin

30. VITIYNLBSIII =30. _____
Just In Case note was left on the ___ cloak

31. WGOINRL =31. _____
Author of the Harry Potter books

32. FUFLYF =32. _____
Three-headed dog

33. OLAFMY =33. _____
Harry's student rival

34. LIFHC =34. _____
Caretaker of Hogwarts

35. AKRD =35. _____
Quirrell's course; Defense Against the ____ Arts

36. YFNDRROGFI =36. _____
Harry's house at Hogwarts

37. TSNISETD =37. _____
Hermione's parents' profession

38. RLOMDVETO =38. _____
Wizard gone bad

39. DIWEGH =39. _____
Harry's owl

40. SGRAHOWT =40. _____
School of Witchcraft and Wizardry

41. ENLVLEI =41. _____
____Longbottom; won points for standing up to his friends

42. RROVTE =42. _____
Neville's toad

43. LOERMDBDUE =43. _____
Headmaster of Hogwarts School

JUGGLE LETTERS ANSWER KEY - HARRY POTTER

1. UTIPENA = 1. PETUNIA
   Harry's aunt

2. RTINSEHYL = 2. SLYTHERIN
   Voldemort's house at Hogwarts

3. EASG = 3. AGES
   Quidditch Through The ____; book Hermione lent Harry

4. EEVSPE = 4. PEEVES
   A poltergeist

5. UQTHCIDID = 5. QUIDDITCH
   Wizard game

6. YRECP = 6. PERCY
   Prefect at Hogwarts;____Weasley

7. ATH = 7. HAT
   The Sorting____; assigns students to houses at Hogwarts

8. YILL = 8. LILY
   Harry's mother

9. EEEKRS = 9. SEEKER
   Harry's role in Quidditch

10. AFNG = 10. FANG
    Hagrid's dog

11. AESMJ = 11. JAMES
    Harry's father

12. SPENA = 12. SNAPE
    Master of Potions

13. URPOTS = 13. SPROUT
    Herbology professor

14. GGMUSLE = 14. MUGGLES
    Nonmagic fold

15. GDIHRA = 15. HAGRID
    Keeper of the Keys

16. IVOAELRDNL =16. OLLIVANDER
Seller of wands

17. SLAEEWY =17. WEASLEY
Harry's close, red-haired friend

18. INCK =18. NICK
Nearly Headless____; resident ghost at Gryffindor House

19. GSOGNTITR =19. GRINGOTTS
Wizard bank

20. CBSBARSE =20. SCABBERS
Ron's rat

21. ROESFT =21. FOREST
Place off-limits to students; Forbidden____

22. EHMNROEI =22. HERMIONE
Girl who applies logic

23. NTIWS =23. TWINS
Fred and George were ____

24. NOEVRN =24. VERNON
Harry's uncle

25. NJAODR =25. JORDAN
Did commentary for the Quidditch match

26. HNSICT =26. SNITCH
Ball the Seeker had to catch; The Golden____

27. SOINRR =27. NORRIS
Mr. Filch's cat

28. OBARN =28. BARON
The Bloody____; Slytherin ghost

29. LEUDYD =29. DUDLEY
Harry's cousin

30. VITIYNLBSIII =30. INVISIBILITY
Just In Case note was left on the ___ cloak

31. WGOINRL =31. ROWLING
Author of the Harry Potter books

32. FUFLYF =32. FLUFFY
Three-headed dog

33. OLAFMY =33. MALFOY
Harry's student rival

34. LIFHC =34. FILCH
Caretaker of Hogwarts

35. AKRD =35. DARK
Quirrell's course; Defense Against the ____ Arts

36. YFNDRROGFI =36. GRYFFINDOR
Harry's house at Hogwarts

37. TSNISETD =37. DENTISTS
Hermione's parents' profession

38. RLOMDVETO =38. VOLDEMORT
Wizard gone bad

39. DIWEGH =39. HEDWIG
Harry's owl

40. SGRAHOWT =40. HOGWARTS
School of Witchcraft and Wizardry

41. ENLVLEI =41. NEVILLE
____Longbottom; won points for standing up to his friends

42. RROVTE =42. TREVOR
Neville's toad

43. LOERMDBDUE =43. DUMBLEDORE
Headmaster of Hogwarts School

VOCABULARY RESOURCE MATERIALS

VOCABULARY WORD LIST HARRY POTTER

No.	Word	Clue/Definition
1.	AGONY	Extreme pain
2.	AJAR	Partially open
3.	AMAZEMENT	Wonder
4.	BABBLE	Foolish talk
5.	BIASED	Prejudiced
6.	BLURTED	Said impulsively
7.	BURLY	Husky
8.	CAULDRON	Large kettle for boiling
9.	CLAMBERED	Climbed with difficulty
10.	CLOAKS	Loose outer garments
11.	CLOBBERED	Battered
12.	CONVINCED	Certain
13.	COWERING	Cringing
14.	CRANING	Stretching, straining
15.	CRINKLED	Wrinkled
16.	DANGLING	Hanging loosely
17.	DESPERATE	Nearly hopeless
18.	DESTINY	Fate
19.	DUNDERHEAD	Dunce, dummy
20.	ELIXIR	Special medicine
21.	ENORMOUS	Very big
22.	ERUPTED	Burst, spewed
23.	EXPELLED	Forced, put out
24.	FASCINATED	Intensely interested
25.	FEEBLE	Weak
26.	FLINCHED	Winced
27.	FLING	Throw
28.	FORBIDDEN	Not allowed
29.	FURIOUSLY	Angrily
30.	FURY	Intense anger, rage
31.	GALOSHES	Waterproof overshoes
32.	GLEE	Joy
33.	GLISTENING	Glittering
34.	GLOATINGLY	In a self-satisfied way
35.	GLOOMY	Dark, dreary
36.	GOBLIN	Grotesque elfin creature
37.	GOGGLE	Stare
38.	GRAPPLING	Struggling
39.	GRUDGINGLY	Reluctantly
40.	GRUFFLY	Harshly
41.	HAGS	Witches
42.	HITCH	Delay
43.	HORRIFIED	Very shocked
44.	HOVERING	Floating suspended in air
45.	INSTINCT	Natural behavior
46.	INTERFERING	Meddling, bothering, in the way
47.	JOSTLED	Pushed, elboweD

VOCABULARY WORD LIST HARRY POTTER

No. Word	Clue/Definition
48. KNACK	Special talent
49. KNICKERBOCKERS	Full pants gathered below the knee
50. LADEN	Burdened
51. LINGERED	Delayed leaving
52. MANGLED	Torn, mutilated
53. MIFFED	Annoyed
54. MUMBLING	Speaking unclearly
55. MUTELY	Silently
56. MYSTIFIED	Bewildered, perplexed
57. OMEN	Sign
58. PECULIAR	Odd, unusual
59. PELTING	Hurling
60. PETRIFIED	Paralyzed with terror
61. PLUMP	Chubby, full in figure
62. POLTERGEIST	Ghost that announces its presence
63. PREFECT	Student officer
64. PUB	Tavern, bar
65. QUAILED	Shrank in fear
66. REFLECTION	Image as from a mirror
67. REMORSE	Regret
68. RUBBISH	Garbage, trash
69. RUFFLED	Disturbed, annoyed
70. SACKED	Fired, let go
71. SAVAGING	Attacking violently
72. SCOWL	Angry frown
73. SCRABBLING	Scraping
74. SEIZED	Grabbed
75. SHUDDERED	Shivered, as from fear or aversion
76. SHUFFLED	Walked while dragging feet
77. SLITHER	Slide, glide
78. SNARLED	Growled
79. SNEER	Scornful facial expression
80. SNIGGERED	Snickered
81. SPECTACLES	Glasses
82. STERN	Firm, severe
83. SUPPOSED	Assumed to be true
84. TANTRUM	Fit
85. TENDRILS	Stems, shoots
86. TIDY	Neat
87. TIMIDLY	Hesitantly
88. TRASHING	Beating, flailing
89. TRODDEN	Walked on
90. TUFTS	Short strands of hair
91. URGENT	Needing immediate action
92. WAFTING	Moving gently
93. WHACKED	Struck, hit
94. WHEELED	Turned suddenly

VOCABULARY WORD LIST HARRY POTTER

No. Word	Clue/Definition
95. WHITTLED	Cut, carved
96. WIZARD	Magician

VOCABULARY WORD SEARCH - HARRY POTTER

```
T P E B I A S E D F E E B L E Y G S G M
I E R R A G X C X E P N A M R N H T O J
M P N E U B P K O P S D O U I U V E G V
I L F D F P B G R W E P F R F D R G X
D U A E R E T L L N L L E F M E F N L W
L M S H S I C E E O I V L R R O M E E J
Y P C C H N L T D N O E M E A D U B D W
R C I N P S F S G H D M G M D T T S F L
I B N I O T Y M T N H G Y O E C E G S K
X N A L L I G U R Y I T K R L A L R A S
I S T F T N C R A N I N G S G G Y U C J
L L E E E C S T S I C D L E N O M F K Q
E I D Y R T R N H T P L S V A N B F E P
Z T D Y G F V A I S E R O N M Y W L D V
V H K J E Z E T N E L B U B A Z C Y I N
V E N T I D Y R G D T S X B B R D G F N
W R A T S K Q D I N I W B N B E L L G T
H S C J T U C E Y N N P W T K I R E N F
A E K D A N G L I N G S U P P O S E D W
C I H I T R R T O V J F C B H K G H D L
K Z L Q T U V S M A T G V A D R A Z I W
E E B P B K K O E S K T G N U H I T C H
D D S N E E R J N Y L S U O I R U F Q V
```

AGONY	ERUPTED	HAGS	PLUMP	SNEER
AJAR	EXPELLED	HITCH	POLTERGEIST	SNIGGERED
BABBLE	FASCINATED	HOVERING	PREFECT	STERN
BIASED	FEEBLE	INSTINCT	PUB	SUPPOSED
BURLY	FLINCHED	INTERFERING	QUAILED	TANTRUM
CLOAKS	FLING	JOSTLED	REMORSE	TENDRILS
CLOBBERED	FURIOUSLY	KNACK	RUBBISH	TIDY
CRANING	FURY	LADEN	SACKED	TIMIDLY
DANGLING	GLEE	MANGLED	SCOWL	TRASHING
DESPERATE	GLOOMY	MIFFED	SEIZED	TUFTS
DESTINY	GOBLIN	MUTELY	SHUFFLED	URGENT
ELIXIR	GOGGLE	OMEN	SLITHER	WHACKED
ENORMOUS	GRUFFLY	PELTING	SNARLED	WIZARD

VOCABULARY WORD SEARCH ANSWER KEY - HARRY POTTER

```
T P E B I A S E D F E E B L E Y G S G
I E R R A     C X E   N A M R N H T O
M P N E U B       O P S D O U I U   E G
I L F D F P B G     W E P F R F D R G
D U A R E T L L N L L E F M E F N L
L M S H   I C E E O I V L R R O M E E
Y P C C   N L T D N O E   E A   U   D
R   I N P S     S G H D M G M D T T S
I   N I O T   M T       G Y O E   E G S
X N A L L I   U R Y I     R L A L R A
I S T F T N C R A N I N G S G G Y U C
L L E E C   T S I C     E N O   F K
E I D   R T   N H T P L S   A N B F E
  T   G F   A I S E R O N M Y   L D
  H K   E   E T N E L   U B A   Y I
  E N T I D Y R G D T     B B R   G   N
W R A   S   Q D I   I       B E L L   T
H S C J T U C E Y N N P   T   I R E N
A E K D A N G L I N G S U P P O S E D
C I   I   R R T O   F     B H   G H D
K Z L   U   S M A T     A D R A Z I W
E E       B   O E S K   G   U H I T C H
D D S N E E R J N Y L S U O I R U F
```

AGONY	ERUPTED	HAGS	PLUMP	SNEER
AJAR	EXPELLED	HITCH	POLTERGEIST	SNIGGERED
BABBLE	FASCINATED	HOVERING	PREFECT	STERN
BIASED	FEEBLE	INSTINCT	PUB	SUPPOSED
BURLY	FLINCHED	INTERFERING	QUAILED	TANTRUM
CLOAKS	FLING	JOSTLED	REMORSE	TENDRILS
CLOBBERED	FURIOUSLY	KNACK	RUBBISH	TIDY
CRANING	FURY	LADEN	SACKED	TIMIDLY
DANGLING	GLEE	MANGLED	SCOWL	TRASHING
DESPERATE	GLOOMY	MIFFED	SEIZED	TUFTS
DESTINY	GOBLIN	MUTELY	SHUFFLED	URGENT
ELIXIR	GOGGLE	OMEN	SLITHER	WHACKED
ENORMOUS	GRUFFLY	PELTING	SNARLED	WIZARD

VOCABULARY CROSSWORD - HARRY POTTER

Across
2. Wonder
6. Foolish talk
10. Extreme pain
11. Scornful facial expression
12. Firm, severe
13. Sign
14. Tavern, bar
15. Silently
16. Intense anger, rage
19. Witches
21. Climbed with difficulty
24. Large kettle for boiling
25. Delay
26. Fate
27. Hanging loosely

Down
1. Prejudiced
3. Partially open
4. Very big
5. Fit
6. Said impulsively
7. Husky
8. Special medicine
9. Nearly hopeless
17. Neat
18. Stretching, straining
20. Fired, let go
22. Burdened
23. Short strands of hair

VOCABULARY CROSSWORD ANSWER KEY - HARRY POTTER

	1		2		3		4			5		6			7		8
	B		A	M	A	Z	E	M	E	N	T	B	A	B	B	L	E
	I				J		N			A		L			U		L
			9		10												
	A		D	A	G	O	N	Y		N		U			R		I
11										12							
S	N	E	E	R		R				S	T	E	R	N			X
	E		S		13					R					Y		I
					O	M	E	N				T					
	D		14							15							R
			P	U	B		O			M	U	T	E	L	Y		
			E			16						L			17		
						F	U	R	Y	M		D			T		
			R				S					18			I		
												C					
			19		20			21	22								
			H	A	G	S		C	L	A	M	B	E	R	E	D	
							23										
			T		A		T	A				A			Y		
				24													
			E	C	A	U	L	D	R	O	N		N				
											25						
				K		F		E			H	I	T	C	H		
				26													
				D	E	S	T	I	N	Y		N					
										27							
				D		S				D	A	N	G	L	I	N	G

Across
2. Wonder
6. Foolish talk
10. Extreme pain
11. Scornful facial expression
12. Firm, severe
13. Sign
14. Tavern, bar
15. Silently
16. Intense anger, rage
19. Witches
21. Climbed with difficulty
24. Large kettle for boiling
25. Delay
26. Fate
27. Hanging loosely

Down
1. Prejudiced
3. Partially open
4. Very big
5. Fit
6. Said impulsively
7. Husky
8. Special medicine
9. Nearly hopeless
17. Neat
18. Stretching, straining
20. Fired, let go
22. Burdened
23. Short strands of hair

VOCABULARY MATCHING 1 - HARRY POTTER

___ 1. WHEELED   A. Special talent
___ 2. SNARLED   B. Growled
___ 3. BIASED   C. Regret
___ 4. BURLY   D. Intense anger, rage
___ 5. DESTINY   E. Husky
___ 6. EXPELLED   F. Tavern, bar
___ 7. SACKED   G. Disturbed, annoyed
___ 8. FLING   H. Fired, let go
___ 9. FURY   I. Turned suddenly
___10. SNEER   J. Throw
___11. KNACK   K. Stare
___12. REMORSE   L. Garbage, trash
___13. GLEE   M. Scornful facial expression
___14. AJAR   N. Said impulsively
___15. WHACKED   O. Large kettle for boiling
___16. CAULDRON   P. Struck, hit
___17. BLURTED   Q. Partially open
___18. GRAPPLING   R. Prejudiced
___19. CONVINCED   S. Fate
___20. GOGGLE   T. Struggling
___21. RUBBISH   U. Meddling, bothering, in the way
___22. INTERFERING   V. Paralyzed with terror
___23. PUB   W. Joy
___24. PETRIFIED   X. Forced, put out
___25. RUFFLED   Y. Certain

VOCABULARY MATCHING 1 ANSWER KEY - HARRY POTTER

I - 1. WHEELED	A. Special talent
B - 2. SNARLED	B. Growled
R - 3. BIASED	C. Regret
E - 4. BURLY	D. Intense anger, rage
S - 5. DESTINY	E. Husky
X - 6. EXPELLED	F. Tavern, bar
H - 7. SACKED	G. Disturbed, annoyed
J - 8. FLING	H. Fired, let go
D - 9. FURY	I. Turned suddenly
M - 10. SNEER	J. Throw
A - 11. KNACK	K. Stare
C - 12. REMORSE	L. Garbage, trash
W - 13. GLEE	M. Scornful facial expression
Q - 14. AJAR	N. Said impulsively
P - 15. WHACKED	O. Large kettle for boiling
O - 16. CAULDRON	P. Struck, hit
N - 17. BLURTED	Q. Partially open
T - 18. GRAPPLING	R. Prejudiced
Y - 19. CONVINCED	S. Fate
K - 20. GOGGLE	T. Struggling
L - 21. RUBBISH	U. Meddling, bothering, in the way
U - 22. INTERFERING	V. Paralyzed with terror
F - 23. PUB	W. Joy
V - 24. PETRIFIED	X. Forced, put out
G - 25. RUFFLED	Y. Certain

VOCABULARY MATCHING 2 - HARRY POTTER

___ 1. DESTINY   A. Assumed to be true
___ 2. SUPPOSED   B. Disturbed, annoyed
___ 3. HITCH   C. Delayed leaving
___ 4. FLING   D. Nearly hopeless
___ 5. DESPERATE   E. Struck, hit
___ 6. BABBLE   F. Hesitantly
___ 7. AMAZEMENT   G. Fate
___ 8. KNICKERBOCKERS   H. Firm, severe
___ 9. WAFTING   I. Throw
___ 10. WHACKED   J. Stretching, straining
___ 11. LINGERED   K. Scraping
___ 12. REFLECTION   L. Silently
___ 13. TANTRUM   M. Husky
___ 14. GRAPPLING   N. Wonder
___ 15. SNARLED   O. Fit
___ 16. MUTELY   P. Special talent
___ 17. CLAMBERED   Q. Full pants gathered below the knee
___ 18. KNACK   R. Fired, let go
___ 19. SACKED   S. Moving gently
___ 20. TIMIDLY   T. Climbed with difficulty
___ 21. SCRABBLING   U. Growled
___ 22. STERN   V. Foolish talk
___ 23. CRANING   W. Delay
___ 24. BURLY   X. Struggling
___ 25. RUFFLED   Y. Image as from a mirror

VOCABULARY MATCHING 2 ANSWER KEY - HARRY POTTER

G - 1. DESTINY		A. Assumed to be true
A - 2. SUPPOSED		B. Disturbed, annoyed
W - 3. HITCH		C. Delayed leaving
I - 4. FLING		D. Nearly hopeless
D - 5. DESPERATE		E. Struck, hit
V - 6. BABBLE		F. Hesitantly
N - 7. AMAZEMENT		G. Fate
Q - 8. KNICKERBOCKERS		H. Firm, severe
S - 9. WAFTING		I. Throw
E - 10. WHACKED		J. Stretching, straining
C - 11. LINGERED		K. Scraping
Y - 12. REFLECTION		L. Silently
O - 13. TANTRUM		M. Husky
X - 14. GRAPPLING		N. Wonder
U - 15. SNARLED		O. Fit
L - 16. MUTELY		P. Special talent
T - 17. CLAMBERED		Q. Full pants gathered below the knee
P - 18. KNACK		R. Fired, let go
R - 19. SACKED		S. Moving gently
F - 20. TIMIDLY		T. Climbed with difficulty
K - 21. SCRABBLING		U. Growled
H - 22. STERN		V. Foolish talk
J - 23. CRANING		W. Delay
M - 24. BURLY		X. Struggling
B - 25. RUFFLED		Y. Image as from a mirror

VOCABULARY JUGGLE LETTERS 1 - HARRY POTTER

1. SAPETDREE = 1. _____
   Nearly hopeless

2. NFIGL = 2. _____
   Throw

3. RNRKEOESBKCIKC = 3. _____
   Full pants gathered below the knee

4. GABBCRSNIL = 4. _____
   Scraping

5. DIEFFM = 5. _____
   Annoyed

6. EEGL = 6. _____
   Joy

7. IGSGAVNA = 7. _____
   Attacking violently

8. NAIGLGDN = 8. _____
   Hanging loosely

9. EFISDTYIM = 9. _____
   Bewildered, perplexed

10. USFTT =10. _____
    Short strands of hair

11. ASLCKO =11. _____
    Loose outer garments

12. SPCAESTCEL =12. _____
    Glasses

13. GGGEOL =13. _____
    Stare

14. HLDEEWE =14. _____
    Turned suddenly

15. LSEOTJD =15. _____
    Pushed, elbowed

16. NMGULIBM   =16. _____
                           Speaking unclearly

17. SLOESHAG   =17. _____
                           Waterproof overshoes

18. ECRNLKID   =18. _____
                           Wrinkled

19. TERENIFLCO   =19. _____
                           Image as from a mirror

20. RIGPLPNGA   =20. _____
                           Struggling

21. DNERTOD   =21. _____
                           Walked on

22. NNGIRCA   =22. _____
                           Stretching, straining

23. DFHENCIL   =23. _____
                           Winced

24. NIVHRGEO   =24. _____
                           Floating suspended in air

25. GITGNSNELI   =25. _____
                           Glittering

26. TEUNRG   =26. _____
                           Needing immediate action

27. NGGGRULDIY   =27. _____
                           Reluctantly

28. ERESN   =28. _____
                           Scornful facial expression

29. BUP   =29. _____
                           Tavern, bar

30. IROSUFUYL   =30. _____
                           Angrily

31. EPCRETF   =31. _____
                           Student officer

32. NDERLSA =32. _____
Growled

33. NETINFEGRIR =33. _____
Meddling, bothering, in the way

34. RETLBDU =34. _____
Said impulsively

35. SDYEINT =35. _____
Fate

36. TSTNCINI =36. _____
Natural behavior

37. CSWLO =37. _____
Angry frown

38. LHITRES =38. _____
Slide, glide

39. FEELEB =39. _____
Weak

40. CKKNA =40. _____
Special talent

41. ELBCODEBR =41. _____
Battered

42. ASDKEC =42. _____
Fired, let go

43. XLRIIE =43. _____
Special medicine

44. CHITH =44. _____
Delay

45. KAWCHDE =45. _____
Struck, hit

46. SRENDLTI =46. _____
Stems, shoots

47. FHFSLEUD =47. _____
Walked while dragging feet

VOCABULARY JUGGLE LETTERS 1 ANSWER KEY - HARRY POTTER

1. SAPETDREE = 1. DESPERATE
   Nearly hopeless

2. NFIGL = 2. FLING
   Throw

3. RNRKEOESBKCIKC = 3. KNICKERBOCKERS
   Full pants gathered below the knee

4. GABBCRSNIL = 4. SCRABBLING
   Scraping

5. DIEFFM = 5. MIFFED
   Annoyed

6. EEGL = 6. GLEE
   Joy

7. IGSGAVNA = 7. SAVAGING
   Attacking violently

8. NAIGLGDN = 8. DANGLING
   Hanging loosely

9. EFISDTYIM = 9. MYSTIFIED
   Bewildered, perplexed

10. USFTT =10. TUFTS
    Short strands of hair

11. ASLCKO =11. CLOAKS
    Loose outer garments

12. SPCAESTCEL =12. SPECTACLES
    Glasses

13. GGGEOL =13. GOGGLE
    Stare

14. HLDEEWE =14. WHEELED
    Turned suddenly

15. LSEOTJD =15. JOSTLED
    Pushed, elbowed

16. NMGULIBM =16. MUMBLING
Speaking unclearly

17. SLOESHAG =17. GALOSHES
Waterproof overshoes

18. ECRNLKID =18. CRINKLED
Wrinkled

19. TERENIFLCO =19. REFLECTION
Image as from a mirror

20. RIGPLPNGA =20. GRAPPLING
Struggling

21. DNERTOD =21. TRODDEN
Walked on

22. NNGIRCA =22. CRANING
Stretching, straining

23. DFHENCIL =23. FLINCHED
Winced

24. NIVHRGEO =24. HOVERING
Floating suspended in air

25. GITGNSNELI =25. GLISTENING
Glittering

26. TEUNRG =26. URGENT
Needing immediate action

27. NGGGRULDIY =27. GRUDGINGLY
Reluctantly

28. ERESN =28. SNEER
Scornful facial expression

29. BUP =29. PUB
Tavern, bar

30. IROSUFUYL =30. FURIOUSLY
Angrily

31. EPCRETF =31. PREFECT
Student officer

32. NDERLSA	=32.	SNARLED
		Growled
33. NETINFEGRIR	=33.	INTERFERING
		Meddling, bothering, in the way
34. RETLBDU	=34.	BLURTED
		Said impulsively
35. SDYEINT	=35.	DESTINY
		Fate
36. TSTNCINI	=36.	INSTINCT
		Natural behavior
37. CSWLO	=37.	SCOWL
		Angry frown
38. LHITRES	=38.	SLITHER
		Slide, glide
39. FEELEB	=39.	FEEBLE
		Weak
40. CKKNA	=40.	KNACK
		Special talent
41. ELBCODEBR	=41.	CLOBBERED
		Battered
42. ASDKEC	=42.	SACKED
		Fired, let go
43. XLRIIE	=43.	ELIXIR
		Special medicine
44. CHITH	=44.	HITCH
		Delay
45. KAWCHDE	=45.	WHACKED
		Struck, hit
46. SRENDLTI	=46.	TENDRILS
		Stems, shoots
47. FHFSLEUD	=47.	SHUFFLED
		Walked while dragging feet

VOCABULARY JUGGLE LETTERS 2 - HARRY POTTER

1. DHRFORIEI = 1. _____
   Very shocked

2. MARELDBEC = 2. _____
   Climbed with difficulty

3. DPLEEXEL = 3. _____
   Forced, put out

4. DPITERFEI = 4. _____
   Paralyzed with terror

5. NESRT = 5. _____
   Firm, severe

6. NATTRUM = 6. _____
   Fit

7. AEBBLB = 7. _____
   Foolish talk

8. RHIANGST = 8. _____
   Beating, flailing

9. EDIZES = 9. _____
   Grabbed

10. SAHG =10. _____
    Witches

11. NLGMEDA =11. _____
    Torn, mutilated

12. CDASFINATE =12. _____
    Intensely interested

13. RFYU =13. _____
    Intense anger, rage

14. GWFAITN =14. _____
    Moving gently

15. AQIELUD =15. _____
    Shrank in fear

16. PLUMP =16. _____
Chubby, full in figure

17. SPOSDPEU =17. _____
Assumed to be true

18. UFGRYFL =18. _____
Harshly

19. UNOEROMS =19. _____
Very big

20. IBSRBUH =20. _____
Garbage, trash

21. YNAOG =21. _____
Extreme pain

22. ARAJ =22. _____
Partially open

23. LHWETITD =23. _____
Cut, carved

24. IMDTLYI =24. _____
Hesitantly

25. DUEDSHDER =25. _____
Shivered, as from fear or aversion

26. ELFDRUF =26. _____
Disturbed, annoyed

27. MOYOLG =27. _____
Dark, dreary

28. EMATAZMNE =28. _____
Wonder

29. ORLTPITEGES =29. _____
Ghost that announces its presence

30. SRMROEE =30. _____
Regret

31. ROECIGNW =31. _____
Cringing

32. ALNED =32. _____
Burdened

33. LYRBU =33. _____
Husky

34. TUEDERP =34. _____
Burst, spewed

35. SBEDIA =35. _____
Prejudiced

36. ERNLIGDE =36. _____
Delayed leaving

37. LETPING =37. _____
Hurling

38. YGTNGOLLAI =38. _____
In a self-satisfied way

39. NMEO =39. _____
Sign

40. DOCUARLN =40. _____
Large kettle for boiling

41. TELYUM =41. _____
Silently

42. CNOEINVCD =42. _____
Certain

43. LGIOBN =43. _____
Grotesque elfin creature

44. RIDNGEESG =44. _____
Snickered

VOCABULARY JUGGLE LETTERS 2 ANSWER KEY - HARRY POTTER

1. DHRFORIEI = 1. HORRIFIED
   Very shocked

2. MARELDBEC = 2. CLAMBERED
   Climbed with difficulty

3. DPLEEXEL = 3. EXPELLED
   Forced, put out

4. DPITERFEI = 4. PETRIFIED
   Paralyzed with terror

5. NESRT = 5. STERN
   Firm, severe

6. NATTRUM = 6. TANTRUM
   Fit

7. AEBBLB = 7. BABBLE
   Foolish talk

8. RHIANGST = 8. TRASHING
   Beating, flailing

9. EDIZES = 9. SEIZED
   Grabbed

10. SAHG = 10. HAGS
    Witches

11. NLGMEDA = 11. MANGLED
    Torn, mutilated

12. CDASFINATE = 12. FASCINATED
    Intensely interested

13. RFYU = 13. FURY
    Intense anger, rage

14. GWFAITN = 14. WAFTING
    Moving gently

15. AQIELUD = 15. QUAILED
    Shrank in fear

16. PLUMP =16. PLUMP
Chubby, full in figure

17. SPOSDPEU =17. SUPPOSED
Assumed to be true

18. UFGRYFL =18. GRUFFLY
Harshly

19. UNOEROMS =19. ENORMOUS
Very big

20. IBSRBUH =20. RUBBISH
Garbage, trash

21. YNAOG =21. AGONY
Extreme pain

22. ARAJ =22. AJAR
Partially open

23. LHWETITD =23. WHITTLED
Cut, carved

24. IMDTLYI =24. TIMIDLY
Hesitantly

25. DUEDSHDER =25. SHUDDERED
Shivered, as from fear or aversion

26. ELFDRUF =26. RUFFLED
Disturbed, annoyed

27. MOYOLG =27. GLOOMY
Dark, dreary

28. EMATAZMNE =28. AMAZEMENT
Wonder

29. ORLTPITEGES =29. POLTERGEIST
Ghost that announces its presence

30. SRMROEE =30. REMORSE
Regret

31. ROECIGNW =31. COWERING
Cringing

32. ALNED =32. LADEN
Burdened

33. LYRBU =33. BURLY
Husky

34. TUEDERP =34. ERUPTED
Burst, spewed

35. SBEDIA =35. BIASED
Prejudiced

36. ERNLIGDE =36. LINGERED
Delayed leaving

37. LETPING =37. PELTING
Hurling

38. YGTNGOLLAI =38. GLOATINGLY
In a self-satisfied way

39. NMEO =39. OMEN
Sign

40. DOCUARLN =40. CAULDRON
Large kettle for boiling

41. TELYUM =41. MUTELY
Silently

42. CNOEINVCD =42. CONVINCED
Certain

43. LGIOBN =43. GOBLIN
Grotesque elfin creature

44. RIDNGEESG =44. SNIGGERED
Snickered

www.ingramcontent.com/pod-product-compliance
Lightning Source LLC
Chambersburg PA
CBHW051404070526
44584CB00023B/3290